MARY'S CALL

THE VOICE
WITHIN YOUR SOUL

*A Daily Spiritual Journal Inspired
by the Blessed Mother Mary*

By Linda Morales

Library of Congress Cataloging-in-Publishing Data

Morales, Linda
Mary's Call: The Voice Within Your Soul

p. cm.

ISBN 978-0-9999021-0-3

1. Virgin Mary—Blessings 2.Prayer—Daily Devotions 3. Spiritual Enlightenment—Religious Aspects and Beliefs 4. Catholicism—Catechism and Conscience

BT 645 C53 2020   232.91 Mo

10 9 8 7 6 5 4 3 2

CANTICLE OF MARY
(LUKE 1:46-55)*

My soul proclaims the greatness of the Lord;
My spirit rejoices in God my savior.

For he has looked upon his handmaid's lowliness;
Behold, from now on will all ages call me blessed.

The Mighty One has done great things for me,
And holy is his name.

His mercy is from age to age
To those who fear him.

He has shown might with his arm,
Dispersed the arrogant of mind and heart.

He has thrown down the rulers from
Their thrones but lifted up the lowly.

The hungry he has filled with good things;
The rich he has sent away empty.

He has helped Israel his servant,
Remembering his mercy,

According to his promise to our fathers,
To Abraham and to his descendants forever.

* Canticle of Mary (Luke 1:46-55) * from the New American Bible, St. Joseph's medium size Edition, Canticle of Mary (Luke 1:46-55)* Copyright@1992, 1987, 1980, 1970

MARY'S CALL

THE VOICE
WITHIN YOUR SOUL

*A Daily Spiritual Journal Inspired
by the Blessed Mother Mary*

DEDICATION

Dedicated to all who want to reawaken
their hearts to the truth that
God Truly Does Exist.

ҬOREWORD

Linda Morales has created, with the help of our Lady, an amazing little book of daily quotes that can inspire and heal us.

Over the last three years I have prayed some of these prayers with Linda and our prayer group that meets in her home. So many people in the group have been touched by these writings that we are all lucky that she has had the courage to follow the promptings of the Blessed Mother and organize these locutions in a daily manual.

It is not easy to risk sharing something so personal and so profound. There is always the possibility of being misunderstood by those who may lack the "feel for" or "trust in," that interior voice that beckons to each of our hearts.

The Catechism of the Roman Catholic Church has recognized such an interior voice as that of conscience: "His conscience is man's most secret core and his sanctuary. There he is alone with God whose voice echoes in his depths (p. 438)*." It forms us in the teachings of the Church within her soul, and the mission to share that voice with us.

The really great thing about *Mary's Call: The Voice Within Your Soul* is that it is digestible in little bites. Just a few sentences a day focuses and helps us walk with the gentleness and motherly care of Our Lady, taking her into the moments of our great joys and sorrows that occur in all our lives.

May Mother Mary bless those who read and meditate upon Her words here, and may we all be given the courage to follow God's will in our Lives!

WRITTEN AT "HEAVEN'S GATE"
IN HEAVEN'S EMBRACE
June 20th, 2017
FR. RICHARD J. BRETONE (FOUNDER)
Eternal Flame of Hope Ministries

*The Catechism of the Roman Catholic Church copyright@1994 Libreria Editrice Vaticana, Citta del Vaticano, page 438, Article 6, *Moral Conscience*, no. 1776.

INTRODUCTION

My life radically changed from May to July 2003. America still mourned those lost on September 11, 2001. I, too, mourned. While many families had grown closer during this terrorizing time, my husband and I hadn't.

"Life's too short," he told me. A month after the towers fell, he moved out and got his own apartment, leaving behind his wife, his son, and his house. When I was growing up, the widows in my neighborhood wore black for years. So I, too, wore black during this time. I wasn't a widow, but I was separated; I was getting divorced. I was lost and I was empty. The world went on, but my aching soul was searching.

I found myself renewing a lifelong devotion to the Blessed Mother Mary. Trusting in her with all my heart, I prayed the rosary daily. Even amid sorrow and anger, even in my moments of despair, she heard me. Mother Mary was already weaving her way into my life, but I didn't know it at the time.

After my divorce was finalized, ending a twelve-year marriage, I went on a Mother's Day weekend spiritual retreat for women at Mount Alvernia in Wappingers Falls, New York. There I met John Trainor and Henry Hudson, who ran the retreat. We women were asked to go outside and write a prayer to the God of our understanding. I sat on a bench next to a statue of Mary. A thought came to me: *Don't follow the retreat director's instructions. Write a prayer as if she is talking to me.* That was the first time the Blessed Mother revealed herself to me.

I wrote what I heard: "Thank you for responding to my call. Know that I love you and my Son loves you. This is where you will find your strength. This is where the love is. Jesus is inside you already. Seek no more. This is the beginning of all the gifts and graces that can be yours if you so choose them. Love is ever-lasting and powerful. It is inside you already. Let the love embrace your heart for you are so deserving of it."

Suddenly a big black bumblebee whooshed toward me. I jumped up and looked at the bright, blue, beautiful sky. Above the statue of Mary hovered a huge round gray cloud, surrounded by a rainbow. I knew in my heart it was a sign from heaven, from Mary. I ran as fast as I could to show the other women but they were too far away.

I reached John Trainor, our retreat director, though. I told him about the visions of the sun spinning and miracles in the sky that took place when the Blessed Mother appeared in Medjugorje in Bosnia-Herzegovina.

"Look at the sky right now," I told him. "Tell me if I'm crazy."

He looked and his eyes teared up with joy. We ran to the other women and told them to look up. By that time, though, the cloud had started to fade. Some of them glimpsed it, though. Right there and then, they knelt in gratitude. Mary's real, I thought. I knew then that my life would never be the same.

A month later, after a business trip, I was relieved to know I didn't have to go away again soon. I could stay home, relax, and hang out at the beach. One late Friday afternoon, I browsed the Internet to look up explanations of the cloud and rainbow. I found none. Suddenly, though, a site popped up for a trip—a pilgrimage to Medjugorje!

I found the courage to call the number listed and inquired. I didn't have the funds to travel because of divorce expenses. I also was refinancing my house. I asked about the cost, anyway. The trip organizer took my name and told me to pray on it.

"No pressure," she said. "Let us know on Monday whether you want one of these last seats."

The trip was scheduled for July. When I hung up, I realized I'd missed a call from the lawyers handling the closing on refinancing my house. They said I was late on choosing a closing date and I should call them as soon as possible. What lawyer calls anyone at 5:30 p.m. Friday on a sunny June day?

The following week, I attended the closing and discovered the banks had made a mistake on my paperwork; they owed me money. That meant I didn't have to make my July mortgage payment. At that moment I knew that the Blessed Mother was providing the funds for my trip and taking care of my home while I was away. I believe that was a miracle. I believe the Blessed Mother was inviting me to visit this oasis of peace.

In my quest for true divine love, I took my first pilgrimage to Medjugorje—and, over time, seven more. I found a peace and connection with the Blessed Mother and Jesus I'd never before experienced. Back home in New York City, I realized Our Lady was the voice within my soul. I awakened many nights, hearing what felt like loud thoughts in my mind and heart. Someone was trying to tell me something. Feeling an intense deep desire to write all these thoughts, I would stumble out of bed and walk to my desk in another room. In the moonlight I would find a blank piece of paper and write what was being revealed to me—messages I now believe were from the Blessed Mother Mary. Each took only a few minutes to write. Once finished, I went back to bed, always sleeping much more peacefully than I had earlier.

The following mornings I would read the messages and think, *This didn't come from me. I don't write this way.*

When the messages began, I thought I'd gone mad. I went to see Henry Hudson, now a friend and also the staff director and counselor at a local hospital in a very busy part of the Bronx. I figured he could tell me if I was crazy. There was always a lot of traffic outside—horns blowing, people talking loudly. As I read a few of the messages to him, everything around us suddenly got very quiet.

"I think our Lady is present with us right now," I said. "When she is present, it's always very quiet. At least that is what I have been told."

"I'm not clairvoyant or anything," he said, "but I smell roses." I think Our Lady wanted him to believe, too.

Still, for many years, I only shared the writings with a few close friends. I tried my best to hide them, bury them, and run away from them. I was afraid of how they could change my life. I was afraid of what everyone would think. Perhaps I was even afraid I was crazy.

It was only recently that a very close friend helped me realize I needed to keep a promise I made a long time ago. One day, in my heart, I promised the Blessed Mother and Jesus that I would share these messages with all of you. If I died tomorrow and stood in front of Our Lady without having kept my word, I would want to die all over again. I don't want to let down my mother in heaven another day. I knew sharing these messages would require a great deal of courage. But I also knew that, with God and prayers, all things are possible.

I gathered all the messages together, contacted Father Richard Bretone, my spiritual director, and asked him to read them. He said he needed to read them from a theological point of view.

"Pretty good stuff," he said, adding that he was honored I would trust him with Our Lady's messages. I believe she picked him to guide me in organizing the messages into monthly and daily reflections. I've since learned that these messages are called private revelations, or locutions.

They helped me realize God is inside of me already. I only needed to allow the messages to enter my newly awakened heart and let their everlasting love abide in me. I traveled halfway across the world in search of them, only to discover they were right in my heart.

I believe Mary's messages are not just for me but for all her children in the world. I hope you, like me, come to believe more and more each day that God truly does exist.

LINDA MORALES
New York

TABLE OF CONTENTS

I Am Calling You

JANUARY 1

Dear Child,

Thank you for responding to my call. Know that I love you and my Son loves you. This is where you will find your strength. This is where the love is. Jesus is inside of you already. Seek no more. This is the beginning of all the gifts and graces that can be yours if you so choose it. Love is everlasting and powerful. It is inside of you already. Let the love embrace your heart for you are so deserving of it.

Pray, I bless you,
Your Mother

JANUARY 2

Dear Child,

Write for me. Help me build an army of men and women for my Son. Adore my Son. Yours will be the kingdom of heaven with my Son. You will not be disappointed. It will be beyond your imagination. Pray for yourself. Pray for others. Pray, pray, pray for the salvation of mankind.

Pray, I bless you,
Your Mother

JANUARY 3

Dear Child,

Come forward and consecrate yourself to my Immaculate Heart. Kneel before the cross and consecrate yourself to my heavenly Son; that he may give you strength and comfort for the task at hand. Let my words reveal the power and strength of my beloved Son, which comes from the power of the highest, God the Almighty Father. Rest and pray and believe in the power of God's heavenly mercy.

Pray, I bless you,
Your Mother.

JANUARY 4

Dear Child,

The order of your life is being renewed. All will be placed according to God's will; good orderly direction. All your actions will begin to reflect the guidance, love and protection you have already been receiving from above. At first your loved ones may not understand. In time they will come to love you more, because it will allow them to love God more and therefore themselves. The gates to heaven in their hearts will begin to open. Only love will surround you. Many hearts will be touched. Thank you for responding to my call.

Pray, I bless you,
Your Mother.

JANUARY 5

Dear Child,

I know why you have come; to do the will of God no matter what. Thank you for coming and know that I will take care of everything for you. All will be well. All prayers are answered in God's time. You need just to surrender and accept the special graces that have been bestowed upon you. You shall be protected and given the strength to do whatever he tells you. Just listen to the wind as I come through the Holy Spirit like a breeze in the spring time. Pray. I wrap you with my mantle for protection.

I bless you,
Your Mother

JANUARY 6

My Child,

I am calling you. You have already received the resources to come and be with me. I have placed my mantle over you for protection. Be not afraid. All will be done and all will be well again. Don't you see the door to the plane awaiting you with the flight attendant, ready to greet you? On the mountain, you shall receive a special healing. Be not afraid. This is a special place chosen by God the Almighty Father. This is a special time of grace for you and others to prepare.

Pray, I bless you,
Your Mother

JANUARY 7

Dear Child,

You have been chosen to help in the salvation of mankind. Thank you for your willingness. Thank you for opening your heart and soul to the love of my Son. Much more will be revealed in its proper time. For now, trust in my love. Thank you for coming.

Pray, I bless you,
Your Mother

JANUARY 8

Daughter,

What would you give up for a little piece of heaven? Are you willing dear child, are you willing to make the sacrifice so that my Son may walk with you a while, showing you the way, healing your very soul? Some things require much praying and fasting. Will you then, fast and pray for my Son's sake?

Pray, I love you.
Your Mother

JANUARY 9

Dearest Child,

This time is for you. Thank you for having responded to my call. It may feel like a big wave of love has just come over you. Go with it. Do not be afraid. It is the wave in God's plan in the salvation of mankind. Peace be with you. This is a time of grace. There are no coincidences in your change this week. Everyday it's change, change, change, change. Consecrate yourself to my Son and to my Immaculate Heart.

Pray, I bless you,
Your Mother

JANUARY 10

Dear Child,

You now know you are being guided. Believe you are being protected. I protect you under my heavenly mantle. More shall be revealed. Choose joy and peace. Pray, I bless you. Thank you for having responded to my call. If you choose to live heaven on earth, you'll never be the same again.

Pray, I bless you,
Your Mother

JANUARY 11

My Dearest Child,

My purpose here is to tell you that God really does exist. His love is merciful and all powerful. I come to bring peace and joy into your heart as God made you in his image and likeness, so are you made of pure love. Nothing, nothing you do can ever destroy this pure love inside your soul. It is I that, if you say yes, will enter your soul and bring out the love, so deeply buried there.

Pray, I bless you,
Your Mother

JANUARY 12

Dear Child,

With my love, I will renew your ever-precious being. That is what God, our loving Father, would have me do. I shall renew your soul with the love of Christ, his only Son, made too in his image and likeness. If God is love and Christ is love, so too are you love in its purest form. I bring peace, joy and love in this instant.

Pray, I bless you,
Your Mother

JANUARY 13

My Child,

I am the voice within your soul. I have come to ask you to pray. I have come to awaken your soul so you may once again come to adore my son who lives inside of you already. Awaken and give your life to God the Almighty who knows what you need and has a purpose just for you. Obey my child. Surrender to my love. Follow him.

Pray, I bless you,
Your Mother

JANUARY 14

Dear Child,

Listen to me very carefully now as I am your Mother. Through my guidance you will come closer to my Son and begin to see only Christ in the hearts of others. The light of Christ is strong in you today. Stay close to the Sacred Heart of my Son. He loves you.

Pray, I bless you,
Your Mother

JANUARY 15

Dear Children,

I want to bring you, my dear children, to holiness. You will go with him everywhere in the kingdom of heaven. More shall be revealed. Go to confession. Fast. I will help you. I will come. Pray, pray the rosary. Help the sisters of the poor. Help the sisters of life. Pray, pray, pray. You were born to do great things. Don't wait my child. Say yes to the Lord now.

Don't wait.
Your Mother

JANUARY 16

Pray, My Child,

Pray, pray, pray. Be not afraid. Stay close to me. Don't worry. Give your worries to me and my Son. Thank you for responding to my call.

Pray I bless you,
Your Mother

JANUARY 17

Dear Child,

Am I not here that I am your Mother? As promised, I continuously protect you with my mantle. You have been chosen. I protect you. Focus on my Immaculate Heart only and on the Sacred Heart of my Son and all will be well. Thank you for having responded to my call.

Pray I bless you,
Your Mother

JANUARY 18

Dear Child,

I know how much you are afraid. But this is a time of grace! Rest in my Immaculate Heart. Look to me only and I will guide you to my beloved Son, who loves you so much. Listen to him. Do whatever he tells you. Feel the peace I offer you. Accept these gifts for they come from God's pure love for you.

Pray, I bless you,
Your Mother

JANUARY 19

Dear Child,

Pray, pray, pray. You do not pray when you run on your will! You do not think that I see everything, but I do! Give everything to me; I shall settle it all for you. Stay in the light of love. Pray the rosary for it will protect you against the snares of the devil who wants to rattle your mind and heart. Stay close to me my child. I am with you now and always.

Your Mother

JANUARY 20

Dear Child,

Love is a very splendid thing. What you feel now on earth is only a tiny taste of all the love God has in store for you in heaven. Thank you for having responded to my call. Thank you for opening up your heart to this vast journey of love. Seek the love from my Son. Seek only the temple of God the Father and you will discover that you need not seek any further than inside of your heart and soul. It is there that the Lord your Father dwells in you through my Son, Our Lord Jesus Christ. Stay close to my heart. Know that I'm with you.

Your Mother

JANUARY 21

Dear Child,

I wish to enter into this house. I will bless this home. Peace will be with you now and always. Surrender your love to me. Look at me only. The love of my Son already dwells in you. He loves you so much. He knows how much you love him. Allow him to heal you. Open up your heart. He will heal you and all those that are in your heart and all those you pray for. Pray I bless you. Thank you for having responded to my call.

Your Mother

JANUARY 22

Dear Child,

My Son, my most heavenly Son will teach you to live a new life. You will become reborn in his passion; reborn in his love. Follow the truth. Follow his way and you shall begin to understand your life with his, which can never become inseparable. He is in you as the Father is in him. It will be wisdom that will bring you into his light my child. Pray for his wisdom and understanding.

Pray, I love you,
Your Mother

JANUARY 23

Dear Child,

Thank you for responding to my call. Thank you for keeping your heart open. As you can see, when you let me come into your heart moments of joy and peace begin to flow from the heavens above into the deepest depths of your soul. Begin to work for me only. Consecrate yourself to me as I will help to bring peace into your heart and hearts of others.

Pray I bless you,
Your Mother

JANUARY 24

Dear Child,

Many will find purpose here. Many will begin to walk the path of their own conversion. I invite you therefore, my child, to be drenched in the light of my love. I ask for your help in God's plan for the salvation of mankind. Without you the task cannot be complete. Many are being called, but will they listen? Continue to adore my Son as I know he is your strength and salvation.

Pray I bless you,
Your Mother

JANUARY 25

Dear Children,

Be not afraid. Your love is sacred. I wish to guide you in the path of love, joy and peace. Do you not want to get to heaven? This is the way. I am the way. Listen to me. Pray, pray, pray the rosary. This is the only way I can be of help to you. This is the beginning of your conversion process. In getting closer to God you will be able to receive many gifts and graces in order to accomplish the special mission that has been assigned to you. Receive it willingly and you will be rewarded greatly when the time is right.

Pray I bless you,
Your Mother

JANUARY 26

My Dearest Child,

It is my pierced heart that you feel right now; the wound of a mother trying to reach her children and they do not see and choose to turn away. God has asked me to intercede for his children and I continue to call for them for true conversion of the heart. Sadness fills my heart when their minds and hearts are closed to the love of the heavenly Father. Pray, pray, pray for the openness of the heart for yourself and others.

Pray I bless you,
Your Mother

JANUARY 27

Dear Child,

Thank you for responding to my call. Yours is only to say yes and God will do the rest. Allow his mighty hand to carry you and bring you to his divine heavenly place. Open up your heart and he will pour his love and peace inside of you, renewing your soul with the Holy Spirit, breathing in you a new spirit, a new joy, a new heart, so that you may carry on God's most magnificent plan for you.

Pray I bless you,
Your Mother

JANUARY 28

Dear Child,

Where are your rosary beads? Hold onto them as they are the weapon against your Goliath. Each bead represents a tear from my heart for all those children who have not come to believe that God really does exist. When you pray, the water from my tears pours upon you with great cleansing of your soul and blessings pouring down from heaven. Dear child, pick up your stones against your Goliath and you will help change the face of the earth.

Pray I bless you,
Your Mother

JANUARY 29

My Child,

Pray. I bless you. Thank you for thanking God for sending me to you. I really do come. Come closer to my Immaculate Heart and to the Sacred Heart of my Son, so that more can be revealed to you. Yes, many graces were poured upon you, so you may continue to do his work. I will always be with you. Be not afraid. Let the Holy Spirit guide you with his love. Embrace my Son for he loves you so much. I love you and keep you protected under my mantle.

Pray I bless you,
Your Mother

JANUARY 30

Dear Child,

Your mission has not yet been revealed to you.

Pray I bless you,
Your Mother

JANUARY 31

Dear Child,

You were meant to touch the hearts of many. You will have new assignments for the New Year. More shall be revealed. It will be clearer.

Pray I bless you,
Your Mother

I AM YOUR MOTHER

FEBRUARY 1

Dear Child,

I am the Mother of light. I am the Mother of all truth. I am your Mother. I am calling you. Come forward and pray with me. Become an instrument of the most heavenly peace and experience the love of my Son in your heart, the love of the Almighty God who only wants the best for all. See the light enter the darkness of your soul and make it anew!

Pray, I bless you,
Your Mother

FEBRUARY 2

Dear Child,

I've come so that many can believe. It will be through your healing that many will come to believe. Do you want to be healed my child? Then open up your heart to me.

Pray, I bless you,
Your Mother

FEBRUARY 3

Dear Child,

You did not choose my Son. My Son chose you. With each prayer that you make, your heart is purified in preparation for all my Son has to give you. He wishes to give you all the love you've been yearning for so long. Let him love you. Trust in him. God's love is perfect.

Blessed Mother.

FEBRUARY 4

My Child,

Thank you for giving your life to Christ, my Son. Thank you for giving your life to my Immaculate Heart. Angels from heaven rejoice in your decision to love your God with all your heart, with all your soul. God's mercy reigns in your soul. His love is the perfect love. Wait upon the Lord for he loves you so. You shall not be forgotten in heaven!

Pray, I bless you,
Your Mother

FEBRUARY 5

Dearest Child,

I wish to heal this home. I wish to enter this home and bring the light of my Son into this home. And God so loved the world he gave his only begotten Son. Place my statue in the kitchen. Become God's servant as you clean. Christ dwells in you. God's love is in you. A house does not make a home. People do. The Holy Spirit will come upon this home and bless all who dwell in it because Christ my Son now dwells in you.

Pray, I bless you,
Your Mother

FEBRUARY 6

Dear Child,

Your light, your heart brings peace to the lives of others and when you enter a home, chaos and darkness are removed and peace, serenity and God enters into the homes of others bringing joy, peace and love. My loving child, pray for your belief and say yes! All you have to say is, "Yes, I believe, help my unbelief." I am already showing you the way. Grace be with you.

Pray, I love you.
Your Mother

FEBRUARY 7

Dear Child,

Be not afraid that they might think you're crazy. If they think you're crazy, stay crazy. In their hearts, they will know the truth. In their hearts, they too have been chosen to walk the path of love and they will only recognize that love. You heard the birds? They sing a song for you from heaven. Smile my child, as I know my love for you gives you great joy! You belong to me.

Pray, I love you.
Your Mother

FEBRUARY 8

My Dearest Child,

So often we wonder if we can do the things that are being asked of us. I tell you the only requirement is your willingness to look into my Immaculate Heart and embrace it with all your heart. Look to my eyes only and I will help bring you to my beloved Son who will guide you in your ways. The only request is for you to say "yes" at this very moment and let go of the results. Everything else will fall into place.

Pray, I bless you,
Your Mother

FEBRUARY 9

Dear Child,

It is only when you surrender that the Lord really begins to work. Miracles happen. Don't you believe in miracles? Give me all your worries and let the light begin to heal you. Give all your sense of responsibility to the Lord and he will begin to be the driver in your life and lead you in the way that God the Father would have it; in his perfect love.

Pray, I bless you,
Your Mother

FEBRUARY 10

Dear Child,

*A*dore my Son. He loves you so much! He is so happy that you love him and want to be with him. You will not regret the choice that you have made; a decision to choose love. A decision to turn your life over to your loving Father brings great joy to all the angels and saints in heaven. You cannot see them but they are all around you. I protect you as always with my heavenly mantle. I surround you with my love. Peace be with you today and always.

Pray, I bless you,
Your Mother

FEBRUARY 11

Dear Child,

*S*o, happy that you've come; that you have come to be closer to my Son who loves you and wants to give you all the peace and love that you so deserve. You are most deserving of it. Stay close to my Immaculate Heart. God the Almighty has great things in store for you. You are blessed. Count your blessings. All will be well. We are with you.

I love you,
Your Mother

FEBRUARY 12

Dear Child,

As you now have come to realize, it is a very special gift to be able to write. I thank you for opening up your heart to me and writing the things I tell you. I shall help you and guide you every step of the way. Be not afraid of what you will write as the words will flow like the river of Jordan through the Holy Spirit and into your soul. And when it is read by the hearts of many, souls will be healed with the tears of joy coming down from heaven. My sweet angel, let the scent of roses come down from heaven and fill your senses. Let it fill the page with words from heaven. Thank you for having responded to my call.

Your Mother

FEBRUARY 13

Dear Child,

Thank you for responding to my call. I call you. I call you by your name. Spend some time with me for I will lead you to my Son. I will lead you to his most Sacred Heart. There you will find the peace that you seek. There you will know his love, his truth, his peace.

Pray, my child, I love you,
Your Mother

FEBRUARY 14

Dear Child,

The temple of your soul is your sanctuary. That is where I come to fill you with graces given me by the most heavenly Father, who calls you to do his will. He calls you to be loving and kind to all who come to do his will; to those who come to ask for mercy.

Pray, I bless you,
Your Mother

FEBRUARY 15

Dear Child,

I need you to begin to pray the rosary. It is when you call my name that I can protect you with such joy and peace so that you can join in the light of the love of my Son. Pray, I bless you. Thank you for responding to my call.

Blessed Mother

FEBRUARY 16

My Dearest Child,

Repeat, "I believe, help my unbelief" and I can then help soften the hearts of my children for the purposes of salvation. Your tears are my tears at this moment. Thank you for having responded to my call. Be not afraid for I am with you.

Your Mother

FEBRUARY 17

Dear Child,

From now on I am going to protect you with my mantle. Dear child, you are so often misunderstood; that is because your heart is so pure and childlike; the way the world takes advantage of those hearts that are pure and trusting. Once a heart is open to the goodness of all, it needs the most heavenly protection, in order to do this. In order for me to protect you with my mantle, I need you to begin to depend on me like a Mother.

Pray, I bless you,
Your Mother

FEBRUARY 18

Dearest Children,

So where do you begin? Where do you begin to learn about all these emotions? It is in entering my school of love that you will learn the greatest of all emotions and that is love. Love is the essence of all things, of all creations. It is through love that you will receive the greatest of joy in your hearts.

Pray, I bless you,
Your Mother

FEBRUARY 19

Dear Child,

Pray the rosary. When you pray the rosary, I come and take away all anxiety. Give me all your worries and I shall resolve everything for you. I invite you to your conversion and way to holiness. I am your mother who loves you. I shall protect you with my heavenly mantle. Thank you for responding to my call.

Your Mother

FEBRUARY 20

Dearest Child,

For he so loved the world that he gave his only begotten Son. Are you willing to walk through the desert for the sake of my Son? It will be a time of reflection, a time of prayer, penance and purification and preparation. For forty days, my Son will carry you through the desert. His will be the only footprints that you'll see.

Pray, I bless you,
Your Mother

FEBRUARY 21

Dear Child,

Hold onto my heavenly mantle as I protect you with my most precious golden cloth. Thank you for adoring my Son. Invoke the help of the Holy Spirit to keep your mind and soul holy. Think of me only and I will continue to guide you towards my Son and the path of the heavenly Father.

I bless you,
Your Mother

FEBRUARY 22

My Child,

Follow the path of my Son, Jesus Christ. He walked the earth with nothing but faith, in the love of his heavenly Father, knowing that all would be provided. As God cared for his heavenly Son, so shall he provide all that you need. As on earth, as in heaven, God the Almighty Father loves you and only wants you to be happy and share in his magnificent love. Look up to the skies and soak in his love.

Pray, I love you,
Your Mother

FEBRUARY 23

Dear Child,

There are times when God the Almighty Father commands the winds, commands the skies, and commands the snow to purify the earth. Be still and know that he is God. Pray, pray, pray for God answers all prayers. Know most importantly that he exists and loves his children with all his heart and all his soul. He then commands you, "There shall be no other idols before me. Love the Lord your God with all your might and all your soul."

Pray, I bless you,
Your Mother

FEBRUARY 24

Dear Child,

Like the manna from heaven, God pours down his love from heaven each day through his everlasting word. It will reveal to you what is needed for the day. It will give you courage and strengthen your faith. Fear not for all will be taken care of. All will fall into place. Many will come to see. Many will come to believe. First you must become disciplined in your own prayer.

Pray, I bless you,
Your Mother

FEBRUARY 25

Dear Child,

Bring me my souls. Let me reconcile everything for you. Many will come. Many will be so happy you have made a warm home for their tired hearts and weary souls. They will be renewed and their souls will be washed by the heavenly stream flowing through their hearts as the blood of my Son Jesus Christ cleanses and purifies my children. Be not afraid. Do your best, I will do the rest.

Pray, I bless you,
Your Mother

FEBRUARY 26

Dear Child,

Many will come. Many will be seeking. Many will be weary. You will be able to hear their steps from a distance like the sounds of herd running in the fields. Running to seek the love of my Son, knowing he is waiting for them with open arms, longing to give them the love they so need and deserve. Pray my child. Do not resist my call, my voice, my love, my grace. Embrace it! I am here to help you! Do your best, I will do the rest.

Pray, I bless you,
Your Mother

FEBRUARY 27

Dear Child,

Be at peace. I will straighten out everything. Look to my eyes only.

Thank you for coming.
Blessed Mother

FEBRUARY 28

Dear Child,

Thank God, the Almighty for allowing me to be with you at this time. I love you. I am with you always. Thank you for beginning to write. You will find so much joy and peace in your writing, for it is part of God's plan for you. Through your writings there will be many, many graces granted you. Thank you for responding to my call.

Bless you.
Your Mother

FEBRUARY 29

Dear Child,

like the snow that drifts in the night; that is what I want you to do with your troubles. Let them drift in the night. Let them drift in the wind bringing its cold pure light upon you, blessing you, purifying you and cleansing the storm in your soul.

Pray, I bless you,
Your Mother

SURRENDER TO MY LOVE

MARCH 1

Dearest Child,

You are to prepare your home. Get it ready for all walks of life to come through it. Fix the bathroom so that many may be able to use it. I will help you. Do not worry. Let go and Let God. Be not afraid. Do not hesitate in saying yes to welcoming those that I send you. I shall protect your home. Thank you for opening up your home and heart to the love of your Father.

Pray, I bless you,
Your Mother

MARCH 2

Dear Child,

It is in communion with my Son that the most heavenly graces can be received from the most high, God the Father. I shall help to heal them all in the darkest corners of their souls. Begin to tell them not to fear for I am with them in their darkest moments. I will never leave you. I will never leave them. Pray for one another.

Pray, I bless you,
Your Mother

MARCH 3

Dear Child,

Offer all your sufferings for the sins and reparations of all sinners, for the salvation of souls. Say yes and your willingness alone will save souls. I am with you and protect you with my heavenly mantle. Pray, pray the rosary. It will be your protection against the Goliath. My Son loves you and adores you.

Pray, I bless you,
Your Mother

MARCH 4

Dear Child,

Come to me my child. Kneel before me. Come to me my child and pray. Do not hide yourself from me. Do not be afraid, for I shall give you a sign. I will come to you and stay. I will stay by your side and lead you. I will stay by your side and guide you on your way. You must my child. You must be obedient to your heavenly Father for he waits patiently for your love and praise.

Pray, my child, pray.
Your Mother

MARCH 5

My Dearest Child,

When you are an instrument of peace and turn your life over to me, others around you will begin to wonder what is different. The difference is love. When you have love, God's love in your life becomes alive and fruitful. Go home now and stay at peace within your heart.

Pray, I bless you,
Your Mother

MARCH 6

Dear Child,

You are to surrender your past. You are to surrender your all, your life, for the love of God your Father, for the goodness of all. Let all that does not belong to you be uprooted so that new life may be sown into your heart that belongs only to God your heavenly Father. Pray for your unbelief and pray for strong faith and courage to walk in his path of holiness. Holiness is the only way. Clear the path and you shall see all hearts will follow in his truth, his light, his way.

Pray I bless you,
Your Mother

MARCH 7

My Dearest Child,

Fear is non-existent in heaven. You will become more courageous once you totally surrender your life to me and my Son and the heavenly Father. Know that we will never let any harm come to you. If anything, surrendering your life to the heavens will become a great joy for you. It will be the only thing your soul will know and recognize; the love and passion that comes only from heaven and it will radiate from your soul through your body to others.

Pray, I bless you,
Your Mother

MARCH 8

My Child,

I am with you. It is you that have been far away, but I have been with you all along. Open up your heart and let me into your soul so that I may guide you to the path of holiness; to the path of our heavenly Father. Be strong my child. Take my hand and never let go. I love you and wish for your deepest conversion. Remain in prayer. Adore my Son.

Pray, I bless you,
Your Mother

MARCH 9

My Child,

You are the happiest when you surrender to my love and the love of God. You will learn through the love of God how to trust and love your loved ones. Trust that they are being guided. Treat them as well with the utmost love and respect. Embark in my journey of love and you will learn to trust Jesus more. Trust they are being guided by the Holy Spirit. Listen to him, therefore, let down the walls that blind your heart.

Your Mother

MARCH 10

Dear Child,

Lean not on your understanding. Remember you are in the desert. Right now the Lord is carrying you and healing you and you are only to focus on love; the love of God onto you. He loves you so. For each emotion, give it to the Lord. Let it wash right through you. It is part of your healing. Say, "Lord, heal me," for every emotion that comes through you. Let him take each thought and turn it into love. Love so divine it will radiate through you. As you know, your heart has been opened. The conditions and foundation for healing have already been established. Move forward, don't look back, it will be better than you imagine.

Pray, I bless you,
Your Mother

MARCH 11

Dear Child,

Must I go to all ends so that you will listen? Isn't it enough that you know how much I love you? I am here with you waiting for you to hold on tight to my mantle. I shower you with love and yet you do not listen and see. My sweet child, surrender now to my Son and God the Father for they will take you places you've never dreamed of. Their love for you is so profound and they are waiting for you to embrace their love so willingly. Readiness is the key.

Pray, I bless you,
Your Mother

MARCH 12

Dear Child,

Though I go no one will follow, yet I go, yet I go. You are to move forward and still face the trials ahead. Be not afraid in your journey to love as I go with you as well as my Son.

Pray I bless you,
Your Mother

MARCH 13

My Child,

Know that God has answered many of your prayers. Look in front of you and you shall see the many gifts you have already received. Yours is only to remove the fear from your heart and accept them, embracing the love before you. Showers from heaven filled with joy and peace pour upon your soul as I speak. Say, yes, to this gift of grace and love. Say, yes, to the healing it will bring your soul.

Pray, I bless you,
Your Mother

MARCH 14

Dear Child,

Thank you for coming. Know that all will be well. There is much you do not understand and I need you to take me seriously. There is much to do in God's plan and time is of the essence. All you have to do is say, yes, and your willingness alone is enough to open the gates to your heart and let me in to the deepest corner of your soul.

Pray, I bless you,
Your Mother

MARCH 15

Dear Child,

You will come to know love in a much deeper way by continuing to adore my Son. Many miracles are coming your way for you and your loved ones. It is important to remain in prayer so that all of you will receive the graces the Lord has in store for you.

Pray I bless you,
Your Mother

MARCH 16

Dear Child,

Yet the truth, the way and the light are the only way to receiving God the Almighty's healing of the heart. Open yourself to the light of his healing and receive the graces necessary to make it through each day. God the Almighty Father has sent his only Son to teach you God's heavenly truth; that he loves you with all his heart and all his might. He only wants the same from you. Love the Lord your God with all your might and all your soul.

Pray, I bless you,
Your Mother

MARCH 17

Dear Child,

Tell him I am well pleased with his garden. He too shall plant a rose garden, as a reminder of my love and presence. And as for him, he is my Son. Tell him that I love him and want him to join me in my journey of love. That is what he needs. Love for healing. There will be better days ahead.

Your Mother

MARCH 18

Dear Child,

There are many that wait. There are many souls that will come to know me through your heavenly heart. Open up your heart and let them in. Open up your arms and embrace the love I give. Open your hand, loosen that fist. Take my heavenly hand once again. For I will take you where I've been; to a place so heavenly, to a place of peace and to the innermost being of your purist soul.

Pray, I love you,
Your Mother

MARCH 19

My Little One,

I know that you are sad. You forget sometimes how much I really love you. I am here embracing you with my mantle, protecting you. Fear not but abandon yourself to me and your entire being will be transformed. Do you not see how beautiful you are already becoming because you have consecrated yourself to me and my dearly beloved Son? Continue to pray, pray, pray. Thank you for calling me. Thank you for giving me all your troubles. I will offer all to God.

Pray, I bless you,
Your Mother

MARCH 20

Dear Child,

God the Holy Father loves you, but you must learn to be still and listen to his voice. It comes in a whisper through your heart. He brings your gifts through me. If you do not stop and pray my child, I am forced to give them back. It makes me sad. Let my love and peace come upon you. Listen to him.

Do whatever he tells you.
Your Mother

MARCH 21

Dear Child,

Pray, pray that I may come. How wonderful it is that springtime is here. Do not forget that God the Father awaits your prayer in heaven in order to open up the channel of his love for you to send you his mercy and grace. Sing praise to the Lord. Don't you hear the Song of praise the birds are singing? Sing along with them in praise!

Pray, I bless you,
Your Mother

MARCH 22

Dear Children,

Spring is a time of buds and flowers blossoming. See how they look up to the light of heaven for nurturing? This is how you should be. Enjoy the warmth of the sun which is God's love for you. A new you is blossoming. Rejoice in the love of my Son and heavenly Father.

Pray, I bless you,
Your Mother

MARCH 23

Dear Child,

There are many saints that are with me now in heaven. One of them, remember, is Saint Pope John Paul II. Follow his example, follow the way he loved my Son. Follow his devotion to pray, his devotion to God. You too can live this simple way of life and receive the richness of the kingdom of heaven. My Son adores you. He wants nothing from you except your sole desire to be with him. Say, yes, and he will show you the way. Take his hand and you will never be lost again. It is a gift to be childlike. It is a gift to be a child of God. Soak in his love for you today.

Pray, I love you,
Your Mother

MARCH 24

Dear Child,

Like a flower that buds in the spring and blooms in the summer, this is a time of grace. Your time on earth now is pouring with many graces to help you in God's plan in the salvation of mankind. Trust is the true ingredient. Begin to live in God's eternity as it is your only reality.

Pray, I bless you,
Your Mother

MARCH 25

Dear Child,

Rest my child, rest. Rest upon my heavenly mantle for it is when you sleep that angels come and whisper in your heart. It is when you are still that your soul can hear the voice of God. Rest your soul upon the Lord and he shall give you peace. You are my sweet child. Pray and rest. Pray and rest. I love you.

Your Mother

MARCH 26

Dear Child,

Do you not want to get to heaven? Come to me and give me your hands. Leave everything up to me. I will settle everything for you. All you need to do is say, yes. I will take care of everything. Look to my eyes and I will lead you in the path of my Son. Adore my Son, for when you adore him, God's most healing power comes alive in you.

Pray, I bless you,
Your Mother

MARCH 27

Dearest Child,

There are at least two books (volumes). There are many miracles and graces alone here that will touch the hearts of many and give them great understanding and hope that God really does exist. Your inner revelations will be part of it and they will be guided to the path of salvation, the path to my Son. Thank you for your willingness. Thank you for saying yes.

Pray, I bless you,
Your Mother

MARCH 28

Dear Child,

The second book will be bringing incredible hope to many to love one another and believe in divine intervention. It will help them believe and pray for all their unbelief. Putting one's life in God's hands can lead to many, many graces and miracles.

Pray, I bless you,
Your Mother

MARCH 29

Dear Children,

Put to rest the darkness, the winter of the old you and step forth into the light of love. The journey of love awaits you. Remember the greatest commandments. Remember, Love the Lord your God, with all your heart, with all your soul. And, love one another! Praise be Jesus!

Peace, I bless you!
Your Mother

MARCH 30

Dear Child,

Thank you for coming to the Mass. It does matter. If you follow me, you will learn to be very present with yourself and others. Yes, I know this is a difficult time for you. Give me your woes. I will heal them for you. I will give you strength for the day. Surrender all your worries to me.

Pray, I bless you,
Your Mother

Dear Child,

Go to Holy Mass. Let the spirit of my heavenly Son renew your soul. Rejoice in the mercy God has for you and all his children. Begin anew by presenting yourself to the Lord the Almighty Father everyday so that he may cleanse your soul and purify your heart once more. Rejoice in his love. Rejoice in my Son.

Pray, I love you.
Your Mother

WALK IN MY PEACE

APRIL 1

Dear Child,

You are meant to touch the hearts of many. Entrust your life in me and you will live abundantly in my love for you. I know there are many trials. Give me your weaknesses for it is in your weakness that you will find your strength. I love you. I am with you always, till the end of time.

Pray, I bless you,
Your Mother

APRIL 2

Dear Child,

When you quiet your mind you are able to hear my call; a mother's call truly from heaven. Be grateful that God the Almighty has permitted me to come to you and enter your heart and soul to bring you peace. This is a new world, a new season. Become children of God by accepting his love and accepting the gift of peace.

Pray, I bless you,
Your Mother

APRIL 3

Dear Child,

Tell my children to come. Tell my children to pray. Tell them not to be afraid. I want them to know that God really does exist. He loves all his children and wants them to follow the way to holiness; to follow the way, the light and the truth of my most heavenly Son who loves them so and is waiting for them with open arms.

Pray, I bless you,
Your Mother

APRIL 4

My Child,

Come to me. Come to me now that I call you. Hear my voice and begin to listen to the beat of my heart pulsating in yours. Listen to the drum of the Almighty Father beating in your heart as he calls you by your name. The Lord God Almighty commands that you love only him. Look up and praise his name. Look up and seek only him. My Son awaits your trust. He awaits your hope. He awaits your ultimate surrender.

Pray, I bless you,
Your Mother

APRIL 5

Dear Child,

Decide for me now. Decide for me only. Decide for the love of God, the heavenly Father who created you in his heavenly image. Give everything to me! Give everything to me! Let go of anything that keeps you from the most incredible love you've ever felt; the love that comes from heaven to touch your heart here on earth.

I love you,
Your Mother

APRIL 6

Sweet Child,

I hold you near even during these times of uncertainty. Look at me only. Let me bring you to my beloved Son that wants so much to purify your heart. Pray for healing for you and your loved ones. Unblock the pains of your heart so I may give you the peace and joy you need to carry on. This too shall pass.

Pray, I bless you,
Your Mother

APRIL 7

Dear Children,

Surrender your lives to me. Walk in my light. Walk in my peace. Walk with me. Peace be with you. My Son adores you and is reaching out his hand. Take his hand and walk with him a while and you shall see the grace in your heart will transform your every being. You will become transparent by the embrace of his love and light. We are smiling here in heaven. Thank you for saying yes.

Pray, I bless you,
Your Mother

APRIL 8

My Child,

Pray my child. Pray for your soul to be purified. Go to confession. There you will dig deep into your soul in the eyes of God and purge all that doesn't belong to you. Surrender all to my Son and he will cleanse your soul, so that you are able to hear his voice, hear his call to you. Then you will be able to answer his call of love, my child. Don't wait. Go to the altar of the Almighty and beg for his everlasting mercy. There you will be healed.

Pray, I do love you,
Your Mother

APRIL 9

Dear Child,

I am here close to you. I am ever present in your life. Know that God the heavenly Father is here requesting that you give him the glory for all blessings bestowed upon you these recent days. Graces will be poured upon you to carry thru his will for you. Know that my Son awaits your acceptance of him in your life. Once you surrender, surrender to his love, things will never be the same. The joy in your heart will be so strong; so overwhelming. You will cry with joy to God the Almighty Father giving him the glory for being his heavenly children.

Pray, I bless you,
Your Mother

APRIL 10

Dear Child,

There can be no doubt. Surrender fully to my love. Surrender fully to God's plan for you. Be not afraid. I am there beside you every step of the way. Thank you for responding to my call.

Stay in prayer,
Your Mother

APRIL 11

Dear Child,

Everything you need will be given to you. Surrender to the Lord for he will be your guide on everything. Jesus loves you. So, do I, my child. Thank you for your prayers. Thank you for responding to my call. Continue to stay close to my Immaculate Heart and to my Son. Say hello to him. Give him my blessings. Ask him to pray, pray, pray.

Your Mother

APRIL 12

Dear Child,

Rejoice! Rejoice this day for this is the day the Lord has made! He has driven the darkness out of the earth and brought forth the light of the heavenly Father to bring forth truth and salvation to all on earth! Praise be to all that receive my Son in their hearts today! Praise and sing Alleluia! Glory to God in the Highest, the Lord my Son has risen!

Blessings from heaven to all!
Your Mother

APRIL 13

Dear Child,

Everything you need will be given to you, each in its own time and plan. Trust the Lord. Say, "Jesus, I trust in you." Pray for his wisdom and understanding. It will be through the Holy Spirit that God's work will come to pass.

Pray, I protect you.
Your Mother

APRIL 14

My Dearest Children,

In difficult times, in good times am I not here, that I am Your Mother? Rejoice in the Lord for he is merciful. All will be well. Love one another. Remember your love is sacred. You are being guided and I protect you with my heavenly mantle. Look up to the heavens today with smiles in your heart knowing that healing only comes when things are unveiled. Your souls are in process of purification. I dwell in your souls with happiness.

Pray, I bless you,
Your Mother

APRIL 15

Dear Child,

Emotions are a gift from God the Father. They are given to you in order to learn the lessons here on earth. It is thru the Holy Spirit that the truth of all emotions becomes unraveled. It is in the unraveling, that the truth begins to heal the most inner parts of your soul, so that truth can manifest itself in your physical being. Thus, then you are healed. God is love and he loves his children so much he created them in love, so that they become love and help to create love. You are love made real.

Pray I bless you,
Your Mother

APRIL 16

Dear Child,

Tell my children to pray. Tell my children to pray for my intercession to the most heavenly Father that in prayer they may come to know the graces bestowed on them as they learn to come closer to my heavenly Son and know that his love for them is truly their inheritance for he has risen! Alleluia! Rejoice in his ever merciful love!

Pray, I love you.
Your Mother

APRIL 17

Dearest Child,

It gives me great joy to see you happy! Adore my Son! He loves you so much. Remember time passes quickly my child. Keep your eyes on me and life will begin to flow like a river of love, full of joy and happiness. Pray, pray, pray my rosary, as it will give you strength and protection enough to swim through this immense river of life. Run like a child in the sunflower fields whose flower only survives with the light of the heavenly Father, looking up to the heavens for life. I smile at you.

Pray, I bless you,
Your Mother

APRIL 18

Dear Child,

I am here. I will protect you. I love you. You have so many obsessive thoughts going through your mind you are blocking the love I'm trying to give you. Be at peace. Don't worry. Give me your thoughts and your emotions. I protect you under my mantle. Let me rock you to sleep.

I bless you,
Your Mother

APRIL 19

My Child,

My heart aches for my children. My heart aches for their souls. Bring my children to me. Let them know my love for them is so strong. I am beside them when they call out my name. I am beside them in their sorrow, in their joy, in their tears. I am beside them especially when they pray. Pray my children.

Pray, I bless you,
Your Mother

APRIL 20

Dear Child,

Yes, there are times when your daily struggles may seem unbearable. Be grateful, however, for all the trials and tribulations you may experience even though it may seem that your enemies have placed a crown of thorns on your head with all their gossip and jealousy and mockery. Be grateful for your inner strength as it is a gift from God the Almighty who will deliver you. Pray for your enemies and forgive them for they not know what they do. Pray that they too may come to know God really does exist.

Pray, I bless you,
Your Mother

APRIL 21

Little One,

I know your heart breaks, especially since you do not understand. But all will be well. My Son is with you. Trust in him. I protect you with my heavenly mantle. As the butterfly struggles in its cocoon, this is a time of grace and conversion. Remember, the glory is just around the corner. Love surrounds you at this time. We are all smiling at you. Enjoy it.

Your Mother

APRIL 22

Dear Child,

on't miss the miracle. Where there is love miracles happen. Pray, as I protect you with my mantle made from the most heavenly cloth giving you the strength to love, love, and love. Be happy, joyous and free. Free to love and be in the presence of the Lord in the presence of your loved ones.

Pray, I bless you,
Your Mother

APRIL 23

Dear Child,

implify your life my child. I will help you. Meditate upon the sacred mysteries of my Holy Son and you will come to know his ways and his truth. Your only focus should be heaven on earth knowing God the Father is your everlasting love.

Pray, I bless you,
Your Mother

APRIL 24

Dearest Child,

ome to me my child, and hold onto my mantle. Each time you slip and let go you get caught in the way of the world. Keep your vision on me. Pray, pray, the rosary for it is when you pray the rosary that I come, my child.

Pray, I bless you,
Your Mother

APRIL 25

Dear Child,

Pray to the Sacred Heart of Jesus. Focus on his bleeding heart as the blood of Christ bathes you with strength and protection. He awaits your smile, your glance, your adoration. Humble yourself in the eyes of the Lord as you will be greatly rewarded in heaven. Thank you for coming. Remember, the writings are a gift from me to you. Thank you for listening. Pray, my child.

I love you,
Your Mother

APRIL 26

My Dearest Child,

Do not worry! Give me all your worries and I will resolve everything for you. Thank you for having responded to my call. Thank you for choosing the Lord your God. It is during these times that you may feel like a whirl spin but it is only the greatest transformation happening inside of you. Thank you for adoring my Son as he loves you so much and knows you are on your way.

Pray, I bless you,
Your Mother

APRIL 27

Dearest Child,

The Holy Spirit is very strong. Its wisdom is a gift to help you and others prepare in the way of my Son. What you saw was real; a wall of fear around him. Do not be afraid as this is the time that God wants you to be still and know that he is God. Fear is only existent in our minds. It is only when we surrender completely to the Lord we release the chains of bondage we put upon ourselves.

Pray, I bless you,
Your Mother

APRIL 28

Dear Child,

My Son is with you! Continue to praise him as you have always done! Thank you for adoring my Son! Take my hand now and remember that I love you and protect you with my heavenly mantle. All will be well.

I love you,
Your Mother

APRIL 29

Dear Child,

Make me your priority today and always. Stop and pray the rosary for when you do I am closest to you and can bring you light in all matters. Don't trouble yourself with life's minor details. You live now in the life of the spirit; the world of my Son Jesus Christ who waits patiently for you. Let not your heart be troubled. All will be well.

Pray, I bless you,
Your Mother

APRIL 30

Dear Child,

Thank you for coming. I want you to plant a rose garden. It will be a reminder to you of my presence. I will help you. You should be like the flowers, always looking up at the sky for nourishment. So should you look at the sky for nourishment from God the Father. Water for the flowers is like prayer for your heart.

Pray, I bless you,
Your Mother

BE NOT AFRAID

MAY 1

Dear Child,

Come to me. Come forward. Press your head against my heavenly mantle for I will cradle you with the deepest love. Be not afraid in stepping out and embracing the love I choose to give. This is the love the most heavenly Father has asked me to give you; the love you will come to know and treasure forever. I touch your heart with my purest love. I touch your heart with words of the most merciful truth. Come my child. Come forward. Come to me.

Pray, I bless you,
Your Mother

MAY 2

Dear Child,

There will be many searching, yearning for his love. Give it to them with just a smile. Give them your love. Give them the Father's love with just a warm handshake and a prayer. Take the hand of God and let him be God. Let him guide you and fill your soul with strength, compassion and love for yourself and others.

Peace be with you my child, peace be with you.
Your Mother

Dear Child,

We are here for you. You are so little. You forget so easily that I am with you always. We are with you till the end of time. You forget that just one glance into my eyes gives me great joy to be with you. Wipe your tears.

All will be well,
Your Mother

Dearest Child,

Yes, I am here with you. Even if you do not see or feel my presence, I never leave you. I am here guiding you. Call my name and you shall see how quickly you'll feel the warmth of my presence around you. All will be well. You are like a flower that has not yet blossomed. Love, light and water are what you need to flourish. Prayer will bring these three things to you so that you can flourish in your faith.

Pray, I bless you,
Your Mother

Dear Child,

Water in the form of the Holy Spirit comes like a breeze in the wind when you open up your heart to me my child. Be not afraid as God the Father's love is perfect. You shall see. Grace is already upon you. Rest my child.

Pray I love you,
Your Mother

MAY 6

Dearest Child,

Want to know how to stop time? Want to know how to set the balance in your life? How many times must I tell you to offer all your worries to me? There is no time in heaven, only eternity. All will be taken care of for you. I am here waiting to enter your soul. Open your heart now my child, and let me in. Only love exists in heaven; only love can heal your most precious soul.

Pray, I bless you,
Your Mother

MAY 7

Dearest Child,

Please tell my Son not to be afraid. He has been chosen in a special way to help renew the face of the church. Do not be overwhelmed by all the earthly, mundane tasks. I will take care of those things for you. Thank you for saying yes to the Almighty Father and for giving your life to the service of the Lord and others. All will be well. I thank you for your kindness and goodness to all.

Pray, I bless you,
Your Mother

MAY 8

Little One,

Be not afraid. Pass into this journey of love and you will begin to receive the graces you will need to heal all that needs healing. Begin to pray the rosary. It is when you pray the rosary that I come and bless you. Come close to my Son. Begin to trust in his love for you and you shall see the heavens open up for you through the love of the Holy Spirit.

I bless you,
Your Mother

MAY 9

Dear Child,

Do not let the things of the earth stand in the way of my love. Do not be tested in the least, for the things of earth will roll away like the current in the sea and the flowers of the season. But, my love and the love of the Almighty Father will hold for all of eternity. Stay close to my Immaculate Heart in gratitude.

Pray, I bless you,
Your Mother

MAY 10

Dear Children,

I am smiling at you. Be not afraid for I am with you. At this time you are not supposed to know what to do. That you must leave up to me. Read my messages from the beginning and the answers will come. God loves you and so do I.

Pray, I bless you,
Your Mother

MAY 11

My Precious Child,

o not forget that it is a special grace to be able to write these messages my child. Stay close to my Immaculate Heart and you will not lose sight of your fruits. Continue in prayer. Continue to pray the rosary so that I can flourish your soul with the scent of the heavenly roses. Do you not smell the roses around you? My child, you are very dear to me. I never leave you.

Pray, I bless you,
Your Mother

MAY 12

My Sweet Child,

ive me all feelings of grief and loneliness and pour them into this basket of love I have set before you at this moment. Kneel before me and bow your head in humility and I shall coat you with my mantle comforting you at this time. You have experienced many losses I know, but know that I will never leave you. I am here now as I have always been. Don't you feel the warmth of my presence around you? Be gentle with yourself. Your tears of sadness will soon be tears of joy. I promise.

Pray, I bless you,
Your Mother

MAY 13

My Child,

Put away the noise. Put away the toys of earthly life. Stay with me awhile. Pray with love for me and love for my Son who wishes to shower you with grace and love. Let us sing a tune of love in your heart as you smile upon the notion that yes, we are real. Yes, God really does exist! And praise him for his presence in you!

Pray, I love you,
Your Mother

MAY 14

Dear Child,

Why do you hide yourself from me? Why have you become so afraid? I am here. I am Your Mother. I protect you. I am with you. I am here. I cover you with my heavenly mantle and I reassure you time and time again of my love. Wipe away your tears and come to me my child. You are safe. You are mine. You are my child.

Pray, I bless you,
Your Mother

MAY 15

My Child,

It is when you try to run that Satan has a feast with you. Run only in the direction of my Son for he waits to hand over all his love. I protect you always with my mantle. Return now to God's love, your true inheritance. All else will come to pass in this world, but your Father's love is eternal. Be at peace for I rock you like a child in a cradle. Pray, for the miracle is around the corner. Pray you see it and not miss it.

I love you,
Your Mother

MAY 16

Dearest Child,

Pay no mind at this time in the salvation of other souls. Instead pay attention to the conversion of your own soul. Pray to my Immaculate Heart so that my love and protection can guide you more closely to my Son. Turn your worries over to me and do not be angry at the world for in time all will know that God truly does exist. Leave that responsibility up to me.

Pray, I bless you,
Your Mother

MAY 17

Dearest Child,

Give me your worries. I will resolve everything for you. At this time, however, your eyes should be only on me. I will protect you with my mantle as there is a special mission for you in God's plan in the salvation of mankind. Will you not follow me at this time? Remember, my Son loves you so.

Pray, I bless you,
Your Mother!

MAY 18

Dearest Children,

How many times must I ask for you to pray the rosary? The rosary is healing prayer. The healing power of God the Almighty Father and protection for you lies in prayers. Be not afraid. I am with you. When you pray the rosary I come and bless you. Do not be angry at the Lord Almighty Father for he has done great things for you! God's love is perfect and has a perfect plan for you! Your faith and trust at this moment should be equivalent to the abundance of the love he has already given you. Open up your hearts and let his unconditional love in so that you may be healed.

Pray the rosary,
Your Mother

MAY 19

Dear Child,

Why are you so afraid? Am I not here, that I am your Mother? I lead you always to holiness. I protect you always with my heavenly mantle. Be not afraid for we are with you every step of the way. When you fear, everything stops. When you fear, my love cannot reach you. Have faith my child, have faith in gratitude that I am with you leading the way.

Pray, I bless you,
Your Mother

MAY 20

Dear Child,

My heart bleeds when you do not come to pray with me. My heart bleeds when you turn away. Trust in the Lord, the Almighty Father, that he will never lead you astray but leads you to his heavenly mansion already placed in your heart. Be open to his grace. Open up your heart now. Trust in God for he will never forsake you.

Pray, I bless you,
Your Mother

MAY 21

Dear Child,

Do not worry so much about earthly matters. I will handle all for you. God's perfect plan for you is at work and you will need to stay close to the Sacred Heart of my Son to receive the many gifts and graces needed to realize God's purpose. Continue to pray the rosary my little one. Thank you for coming. I hug you with the wind.

Pray, I bless you,
Your Mother

MAY 22

Dear Child,

The Holy Spirit sends forth the truth and sometimes no matter what you see, it is not important in the eyes of God. What is important is your humility and your own self-worth. Remain humble and still and it will all pass. God the Father will take care of it all. Give me your tears. Hold on to my mantle during this time. This too shall pass.

Pray, I bless you,
Your Mother

MAY 23

Dear Child,

Love always endures. Lean your eyes on me and think of me only. The earthly things will pass before you. Focus instead on the love of your Father. Focus instead on the love inside of you. Peace be with you. Give me your worries. Give me everything. You know I will take care of everything. Pray I bless you.

Sleep now my child,
Your Mother

MAY 24

My Dearest Children,

Remember that you have been chosen for a very special mission. God the Father knows how much you love him. He only sees the love that is in your hearts. As I have told you before, your love is sacred. Rest in each other's hearts, as you rest in the heart of my beloved Son.

Pray, I bless you,
Your Mother

Dearest Child,

Have faith. Take heart. The Lord taketh away all the inequities of your humanness. Everything, everything that has happened, has happened for the glory of God and although you agreed to it a long time ago, your sufferings and your grief has been lifted from you.

I bless you,
Your Mother

Dear Child,

The Holy Spirit came and swept away all your sorrows and made way the path of the Lord; the path that led you to this point, the path to the doorstep of the Sacred Heart of my Son. Hang on to the faith in your heart, for it is a gift. The sun always comes out in the morning and it will be brighter than you've ever imagine.

Pray, I bless you,
Your Mother

Dear Child,

Remember, when you pray you not only pray on earth but also in heaven. Angels wait for your requests and wish to intercede for you.

Pray, I bless you,
Your Mother

MAY 28

Little One,

You are to remain cheerful. You are to remain cheerful, chirping like the birds on your window sill; happy, joyous and free, the way God created you. In this way, others will be drawn to your light; the light of peace within you. As they move closer to the light within you, they will come closer to my Son, for his light is the light inside of you.

Your Mother

MAY 29

Dear Child,

Many live in darkness and do not like the light they see in you but you are to shine among the darkness. Your light is a reflection of my love for you and all my children. Those that hurt inside will be disturbed by it but do not be weary by it. Do not be afraid for you will also bring forth the love and brightness of many others who have come to know my Son. Let your light be a sign of my love for you and the love of my Son for all to see.

Pray, I bless you,
Your Mother

MAY 30

Dear Child,

Pick up your tools against your Goliath. The light in the darkness, the shield, is my heavenly Son who will protect you in your journey as you comfort my souls. Pray always, my child.

Pray, I bless you,
Your Mother

Dear Child,

In forgiveness, all will be re-aligned with the power of God the Almighty and all will be well. Pray for the courage to do whatever he tells you. Pray for the wisdom and knowledge for when action is necessary.

Pray I love you,
Your Mother

Do Not Give Up Hope

JUNE 1

Dear Child,

I am with you. In love, you will learn to trust. You will come to understand that I am here guiding you, showing you the way to my Son. With love, you will no longer need to hide. It will be known that you are my child and I am interceding for you every step of the way. For God and my Son are with you, blessing you, giving you joy every day. We are happy that you are here. Smile my little one. Touch my heavenly mantle and know I come to protect you. Nothing will ever happen to you that you and God the Almighty cannot handle. Be still and know he is God.

Pray, I love you,
Your Mother

JUNE 2

Dear Child,

It is time to enter this journey of love. Pick up your tools against your Goliath. Pick up your rosary and pray, pray, pray without ceasing. Seek God's will for you in his scripture. Open your bible and allow his heavenly words to speak to your heart. There you will find his truth. Be not afraid for the journey will be amazing.

Pray, I bless you,
Your Mother

JUNE 3

Dear Child,

Pray to the Holy Spirit, ask for what you need and then let it go. Watch then how our heavenly Father's love is so perfect and loves you so much. Today, pray for God's mercy. Pray his divine mercy in atonement for your sins and those of the whole world. Pray "Oh, blood and water, poured forth from the side of Christ, sanctify me. Jesus, I trust in you". Thank you for having responded to my call.

Your Mother

JUNE 4

Dearest Child,

Time to get off the pedestal. The pedestal of human nature. Humbly ask the Lord to guide you in your path. Place all your relationships in God's hands. Those that are real will remain. Those that are false will move on. The only way you will know is if you let go and let God. Be not afraid. There is a plan here. You are not in charge. Your heavenly Father is.

Pray, I bless you,
Your Mother

JUNE 5

Dear Child,

Although life is difficult right now, you should not be discouraged. Although it may seem as if you are surrounded by darkness, it is only the still of the night that you are resting in. Little do you realize you are truly the light in the stillness. Yours is only to open up your heart to me, so that I may continue to illuminate your soul with God's heavenly love and lightness. Know that all your prayers have already been answered. Be still my child and know that he is God. This is a time of thanksgiving. Count your blessings. Be happy.

Pray, I bless you,
Your Mother

JUNE 6

My Dearest Child,

Sometimes your plans are not the same as those in heaven. Sometimes on earth things are seen as sadness when in heaven they are seen as glorious. Know that now is the time to accept the graces pouring down on you. Soak in the love and peace and joy sent to you from heaven for all you have done. Know that the love you bore for your Son was like the love I bore for my Son. So deep and so intense was my acceptance to do God's will. As I was rewarded in heaven so you shall be rewarded.

Pray, I bless you,
Your Mother

JUNE 7

Dear Child,

Let those tears rolling down your eyes become tears of joy here in this beautiful garden of love. The birds are chirping to get your attention. Look up at the sky and see the love of God all around you. Feel the breeze of the Holy Spirit as I embrace you with my love. Let not your heart be troubled. Bring back that childlike faith. Put it back in your heart. Open your mind and your soul and let God the Almighty Father do great things in you. Be still and know that we are here.

Pray, I bless you,
Your Mother

JUNE 8

My Child,

We are here by your side. We are here to give you the strength you need to carry on. Lay all your burdens at the foot of the cross and the Lord will give you peace. Peace, peace my child. Stay in prayer with us. Keep your eyes on mine. I will take you by the hand and give you a taste of heaven in your soul to lighten your day. Do you feel it already? I am always with you. Am I not, that art your Mother? Worry not about tomorrow, for God will provide all you need one day at a time.

Pray, I bless you,
Your Mother

JUNE 9

Dear Child,

Listen to me. Stop and pray for the Holy Spirit speaks to your heart and if you do not stop you will miss the guidance of my love for you. Truth comes in many forms and your preparation is crucial in opening up your heart and mind to the ways of the Lord, my Son.

Pray, I bless You,
Your Mother

JUNE 10

My Dearest Child,

Yes. I am here. We have not gone anywhere. We are always with you. It is the thoughts in your mind that run away with you at times. Empty out the thoughts and worries so that only goodness and love you will find. Pray, pray so that your heart can be renewed and re-energized by the love of our heavenly Father who loves you so much and will not allow any harm to come to you. I protect you with my heavenly mantle. Even if you do not see me, know that I am here. Act as if you see me and you shall see that love will embrace you faster than you can imagine. The Father has sent you angels to protect you. They surround you. Pray to the Holy Spirit to give you the strength and peace of mind you need for the days ahead and always.

Pray, I bless you,
Your Mother

JUNE 11

Dearest Children,

As you can see there will be many trials. You are the children of the light. Many souls live in darkness and the love radiating from you is disturbing to them as they have forgotten the light of Christ in them. These times may seem difficult. Humbly remain embraced in my mantle as I protect you. As you unite, your lives will become an eternal prayer. Continue to soak in God's perfect love for you. Thank you for saying yes.

Pray, I bless you,
Your Mother

JUNE 12

Dear Child,

Pray, pray, my child. It is the only way I can help you. If you do not ask for my help, I cannot interfere. Only with my love in your heart and soul can I intercede for you my child. Pray, pray the rosary.

Pray, I bless you,
Your Mother

JUNE 13

Dear Child,

Pray before the Holy Mass. You must prepare before you go so that you may receive God's living words in the most intimate way, straight to your heart. In receiving my Son, you must be ready for his healing and love. Much healing needs prayer and fasting.

Pray, I bless You,
Your Mother

JUNE 14

Dear Child,

Do not give up hope my child. Do not be down in spirit for the miracles are just around the corner. Haven't you seen miracles before you already? Do not be deceived by earthly showings as they are only a deterrent in God's plan for you! God the Almighty Father has done great things for you and has so much yet in store for you. Look into your heart. There you will know the truth; the truth shown to you by my beloved Son. You are not alone. We are with you.

Pray, I bless you,
Your Mother

JUNE 15

Dear Child,

Why do you question my love for you so? Be not afraid. Have courage. I am here by your side always. Your words will be my words. They will know. They will know in their hearts. Tears of joy will begin to flow from their souls rejoicing in the knowledge that they are not alone; that they have never been alone. I am with them always.

Pray, I bless you,
Your Mother

JUNE 16

Dear Child,

Hold on to my mantle. Don't let it go. Do not beat yourself up for that is what the devil wants. Stay humble now and pray that the roses come out from your heart again. Give me your troubles and I will purify your soul. Pray for those you love. Don't be afraid.

Pray, I bless you,
Your Mother

JUNE 17

Dear Child,

Your thoughts and words should only be of peace and love, for I have shown you the way numerous times. And as my Son has commanded you, "Love your neighbor as yourself." In these trying moments, do not forget to look up, and call out my name and the name of my heavenly Son, Jesus. We come, you know, in the instant that you call. You are loved. You are blessed. Count your blessings.

Pray, I bless you,
Your Mother

JUNE 18

Dearest Child,

They do not understand. Sometimes things happen for a reason unknown to those on earth for the benefit of all and change is not comfortable. Treat them with dignity, love and respect no matter what. They are souls that love you in the best way they can and their intentions, although good ones, falter at times.

Pray, I bless you,
Your Mother

JUNE 19

Dear Child,

Be not afraid. I know it seems like the world is falling apart at the seams, but there are times when things happen for our own good that we are not meant to understand. Trust in the Lord your God for he is with you today and always.

I am always with you,
Your Mother

JUNE 20

Dear Child,

I know my little one. It is not so easy to have patience and tolerance on earth but rest assured that God's plan is greater that you can ever imagine for you. Ask for his mercy and wait upon the Lord for he is good and merciful. Someday you'll look up and say how quickly time really flew in heaven and that sigh of relief will be a sigh of much gratitude. Do not give up hope. Be of good cheer.

Pray, I bless you,
Your Mother

JUNE 21

Dear Child,

Although your heart may be pierced with a touch of loneliness, you are not alone. Don't you see? You touch the hearts of many. Reach out to them and you shall see. Reach out to them and you will feel the shift in your heart. With love and compassion for others your own heart can be healed. Pray for yourself and others, for they too have come to pray. They too wish to be saved. You are not alone. I am with you all.

Pray, I bless you,
Your Mother

JUNE 22

Dear Child,

Do not hide your illness; instead become an advocate for its cause, due to many that suffer with you. Offer your sufferings for the healing of all these souls that they too may be healed. Release the shame that binds you as that is part of the illness. Pray often the Anima Christi. Pray, "May the blood of Christ inebriate me and may the water from his side wash me, cleanse me and renew my spirit." Be happy, for I am with you.

Pray, I bless you,
Your Mother

JUNE 23

Dear Child,

I know the pain of sorrow. I know the feeling of a pierced heart. Many a word was said to me. Many a times I cried. But in his glory, I did obey. In his glory, I did arise. In his glory, I saw the light. In his glory, I witnessed his resurrection! Glory be to the Father and to the Son and to the Holy Spirit!

Pray, I love you,
Your Mother

JUNE 24

Dear Child,

What happened to being in seclusion in order to pray and write? The power of prayer is tremendous. God's almighty power is tremendous if you surrender to his will. I am here waiting for your hand so that I may enter your soul and help to bring your intentions and prayers to God the Father himself.

Pray, I bless you,
Your Mother

JUNE 25

My Child,

Please accept which way this is supposed to unfold. Be still and know that he is God. Go in total blind faith and give total unconditional love. You are protected. You are guided. Strength will be given you. Pray the rosary.

Pray, I bless you,
Your Mother

JUNE 26

My Dearest Child,

It is through your writing that I come. Pray that you hear my voice and pray that you do not hide from me. I protect you with my mantle.

Pray, I bless you,
Your Mother

JUNE 27

Dear Child,

Like the river flows, so will my healing light flow through your every soul, your every being, giving you a new breath, a new life. I've waited so long my child, and you have come to answer the call; the call of salvation of the most heavenly Father when you have come to know he exists and loves you so strongly. Declare your life for him and you will never be the same.

Pray, pray, pray, strongly,
Your Mother

JUNE 28

Dear Child,

Can you smell the fragrance of my love in the air? Wash yourself upon the water of my love, flowing in the river so pure, so healing. Many will come. Many will be blessed. Many will be chosen. Many will be healed. Praise the Lord, Sing Hallelujah! Glorify his heavenly name! Sing Jesus, Sing Jesus! Call out his heavenly name! I smile upon you from heaven!

Pray, I bless you,
Your Mother

JUNE 29

Dear Child,

Come follow me, thru the pathway of love. Seek the richness of my love in your heart. Follow your heart for I am calling you. Come and see the place I have prepared for all my children to come and bathe in the waters of my love sent by the most heavenly Father. Love him with all your heart for he is most merciful to you. Pray, I bless you.

I love you.
Your Mother

JUNE 30

My Child,

Be thankful that you have received the gift of writing and continue to send blessings to others for us from heaven.

I bless you,
Your Mother

Do Whatever He Tells You

MAY
Page 95

JULY 1

Dear Child,

s not the Father the perfect Father? Turn back to your Father and look up to him for guidance. He has not failed you yet. It will be better than you imagine. Pray my child. Try to pray. Give me all your worries.

I shall give you peace,
Your Mother

JULY 2

Dear Child,

t is through your writing that your soul wakes from an endless sleep in the darkness of your existence. Praise the Lord your God for he is merciful to you and all creatures on earth. He blesses you in this most precious moment and always. Begin to write again in order to complete the mission that has been assigned to you so long ago.

Pray, I bless you,
Your Mother

JULY 3

Sweet, Sweet Child,

Uncovering the layers over your heart is no easy task. Uncovering the hearts of millions is my purpose here. To help the heavenly Father by bringing awareness to his children that he truly does exist and he truly loves his children. He created you in his image. If he is all love and all good, why would you think otherwise?

I bless you,
Your Mother

JULY 4

Dear Child,

Let the Holy Spirit come upon you and awaken the depths of your heart so that you may help many come closer to the Lord once again. It will become clearer through your prayer and writing that they go hand and hand with God's eternal love. Pray my child. I will always be here guiding you, loving you.

Pray, I bless you,
Your Mother

JULY 5

Dear Child,

All you need to do is ask and the healing will begin in the opening of your heart to me. The Holy Spirit will pour down upon you many, many, graces necessary for you to be healed and, therefore, be an instrument of peace to others. Pray, pray, pray the rosary. It will be the weapon against your Goliath. Thank you for having responded to my call.

Pray, I bless you,
Your Mother

JULY 6

Dear Children,

Stay close to my Son. Adore him for he loves you so much and he knows how much you love him. I want you to join me in the school of love. Your hearts are now open. This is why you feel sorrowful. To be human is painful enough. Be at peace that you are being guided. Say "yes" to the willingness to be healed by our heavenly Father who knows how much you love him. Stay in the path of love.

Pray I bless you,
Your Mother

JULY 7

Dear Child,

MAY
Page 99

We are here. We love you. We protect you. All will be well. Never fear. We guide you into the light and out of darkness. No more tears of pain, only tears of joy stemming from the love and peace of God. From the love and peace of my Son, who is teaching you the truth and giving you the strength and courage to carry on. Be at peace and carry on.

Pray, I bless you,
Your Mother

JULY 8

Dearest Child,

Come forth towards me and give me all your mindless thoughts for they are blocking the healing light that will give you peace. Place all your worries in my hands and I will settle everything for you. The Holy Spirit will guide you. You will know in which direction to go. Trust in my Son. God the Almighty has not failed you yet. He has not carried you this far to drop you now. Smile my child, as I am smiling too. All will be well.

Pray, I bless you,
Your Mother

JULY 9

Dear Child,

Awaken! Awaken! For he will come like the thief in the night. He will come calling and will you be ready? Pick up your tools. Pick up your rosary and be vigilant against the snares of the evil one who wishes to prey on innocent souls. You shall overcome only by opening up your heart again to my most heavenly son! Open up your heart and receive him now for he so wants to heal your soul. Lift up your heart and pray. Lift up your voice to the Lord and pray, "Jesus, it is I. I have come to love you once again. Please heal me."

Pray, I love you,
Your Mother

JULY 10

Dear Children,

I do not want negative things coming from your mouth. Surrender to my school of love. Surrender your life to me so I can bring out the best in you. Don't you see how beautiful you are? It is because you love! Do not shed those tears of sadness. Do not shed tears of unbelief, but pray instead for stronger belief. I have come so that many might believe. Believe that God exists and that many may choose the path to holiness.

Pray, I bless you,
Your Mother

JULY 11

Dear Children,

MAY
Page 101

Do not fill your hearts with anger. There shall only be love in your hearts. Let the love of God the Almighty Father fill your every being so that you may be transformed and continue to be the instruments of peace he set out for you to be. Then you will be true disciples of his love and help to transform the world.

Your Mother

JULY 12

My Child,

I do not want you to worry. I do not want you to guess. Your road, your path will be cleared. Your road will be covered with light at every turn. Do not worry for I am here. Do not worry. I am near. I have settled everything for you. Rejoice in the son of the Almighty Father.

Pray, I bless you,
Your Mother

JULY 13

Dear Child,

You have already been given the tools for healing. Trust in the power of God and be willing to let go of all that does not belong to him for the sake of your salvation and the salvation of mankind. Trust that love has already healed your being and that you belong to God the Divine who will guide you and protect you always. I am with you. I protect you with my heavenly mantle. Be not afraid.

Pray, I bless you,
Your Mother

JULY 14

Dear Child,

You are to listen to me. You are to stay close to my Heart. You are to be vigilant in your prayer. I will fix everything for you. Yours is only to follow my voice in your heart so that I may enter and intervene on your behalf. Be not afraid. I will be with you every step of the way.

Pray, I bless you,
Your Mother

JULY 15

Dearest Children,

Be not afraid. We are with you. Now is not a time to freeze. It is a time to act quickly. Time is short. There is much to prepare. Do whatever he tells you and repeat "Lord, heal me. Jesus, I trust in you". Otherwise you will miss the miracle. The lesson here is unconditional love. You are meant to walk the storm, but in time, you will get past the darkness. It is part of the plan for you, God's perfect plan. True love cast out all fear. Walk now towards the light. See only his love for you and you shall be healed in his light. I am with you.

I protect you,
Your Mother

JULY 16

Dear Child,

Decide for me only. I will place everything in order for you. Look to my eyes for in them is the love I wish to enter into your soul. I shall protect you with my heavenly mantle. The angels in heaven are singing for you, surrounding themselves around you, whispering love in your ears. As this is a time of grace, be grateful to my heavenly Father that I have come. Thank you for responding to my call.

Pray, I bless you,
Your Mother

JULY 17

Dear Child,

Look to my eyes only at this time and I will lead the way to my Son. Here is where you will find the joy and happiness that you seek. Pray I bless you.

Thank you for responding to my call,
Your Mother

JULY 18

My Dearest Child,

Come close to my heart at this time. Take my hand and walk with me for a while. You are meant to be an instrument of peace. It is in forgiveness that all will be well. I will lead the way. Listen to your Mother's heart. It is the voice of reason.

Pray, I bless,
Your Mother

JULY 19

Dear Child,

Walk the path of my love. Feel the breeze upon your face as you look up to the most magnificent light coming from above covering you with rays of light and love. The warmth you feel is the warmth of my heart for you. Thank you for responding to my call.

Pray, I bless you,
Your Mother

JULY 20

Dear Child,

Pray incessantly to my Son for you to see through his eyes only.

Pray, I bless you,
Your Mother

JULY 21

Dear Child,

Refresh your soul with the blood of my Son cleansing your every being. Praise him. Love him for he waits with open arms to give you love in a way you could never imagine. Rejoice in his love for he loves you so. Thank you for responding to my call.

Pray, I bless you,
Your Mother

JULY 22

Dear Child,

Be in communion with my Son first, for he is your shield and your salvation. Go to Holy Mass. Become one with the most high, God the Almighty, and be in communion with my Son. He is your light and saving grace.

Pray, I bless you,
Your Mother

JULY 23

Dear Child,

It is thru the Holy Eucharist that a soul begins to heal. It is in adoring my Son, Our Lord Jesus Christ that all begin to align themselves with God's will. Bring me these souls and I will bless them and help to begin to soften their hearts so that they too will receive the glorious healing of the Lord, God the Father. Begin to pray the rosary more often for my intentions in the conversion of these souls. Tell them to adore my Son and receive him in the most Holy Eucharist.

Pray, I bless you,
Your Mother

JULY 24

Dear Child,

Your daily prayer shall be, "Oh dear Lord, why does my cup runneth over? What would you have me do? I am here seeking; seeking your love, your peace, your forgiveness and your mercy. I am here ready to surrender all my love for all your goodness. God Almighty, I give your Son all the praise and glory today and always. Thank you for choosing me. Thank you for your patience and your most heavenly glory."

Pray, I bless you,
Your Mother

JULY 25

Dear Child,

I have been here all along. I have been waiting for your heart to open. Take courage. Be not afraid. I am here. I will guide you in a path and renew your spirit, bringing truth and purity to your soul as you learn to love my Son again, the way you did so long ago.

Pray, I bless you,
Your Mother

JULY 26

Dear Children,

I make everything anew. I make everything anew. Like the flowers and grass that grow near a river or stream, your souls will grow in richness of the Lord, Our Heavenly Father. Let the stream of love flow through your hearts making everything new in your hearts filling your every being with the strength and love of my Son.

Pray, I bless you,
Your Mother

JULY 27

Dear Child,

When you feel a drop of my love, you will cry. You will cry with joy and praise the Almighty God, giving him praise and glory for his everlasting mercy. Open your hearts now and rejoice! Look up to the heavens for it is real. Seek the truth in your hearts and you will find great healing. I cover you with my heavenly mantle.

Pray, I bless you,
Your Mother

JULY 28

Dear Child,

Stay close to my Immaculate Heart for there is where I can protect you most. I shall wrap you with my heavenly mantle like a Mother wraps her child, in the most loving way. Stay close to me. Call out my name. Call out the name of my Son and we shall come running quicker than it takes to open up your eyes. Be not afraid. No one can break what's coming your way. No one can take the blessings God has bestowed upon you. It is already written in heaven. You are my child. You are God's most heavenly child.

Pray, I bless you,
Your Mother

JULY 29

My Child,

Peace my child, peace. Do not worry about tomorrow for I am with you. When you worry, you block the sound of my voice and then you cannot hear the call of my heart that wants to settle everything for you. Be of good cheer. All will be well.

Pray, I bless you,
Your Mother

JULY 30

Dearest Child,

The Holy Spirit will take charge of your soul and you will be renewed. Thank you for your acceptance and humility. Remain humble with me in the presence of the Lord. You need to remain as silent as possible in order to hear the whispers of the Lord deep in your hearts. You will know. You will recognize his voice. You will be transformed. All will be well. Pray, pray, pray. It is a time for prayer.

I bless you,
Your Mother

JULY 31

My Dearest Child,

I hear your voice. I hear your worries. Give them all to me. Be at ease knowing that you are in the right place. You did not come back the same. You have been transformed and in prayer, your true self is being slowly revealed. Simplicity will be the key to your new self.

Pray, I bless you,
Your Mother

STAY IN PRAYER

AUGUST 1

Dear Child,

How do you pray? Do you kneel before the Lord? Do you sit down in a chair? Do you worship Almighty God while working at your desk? Pray, pray, pray with your heart every second of the day. Call out the name of Jesus and say "Jesus, I trust in you." Ask the Lord to fill your heart with gratitude.

Pray I bless you,
Your Mother

AUGUST 2

Dear Child,

Feel the warmth in your heart that is caressing your soul my child. Know that you are loved here in heaven as on earth. You are going to be okay. Thank God the Almighty for allowing me to be with you here in heaven as well as on earth. I comfort you as well and send you roses from heaven as a token of my love for you.

Your Mother

AUGUST 3

Dear Child,

Stay in prayer. Remember when you pray the rosary, I come my child. In due time, you shall see your loved ones. We will take care of everything for you. Stay at ease my child. Enjoy soaking in our love.

Pray, I bless you,
Your Mother

AUGUST 4

Dear Child,

Pray to the Sacred Heart of Jesus. Ask and you shall receive. Knock and the door shall be opened.

Pray, I bless you,
Your Mother

AUGUST 5

Dear Child,

Believe then that you already have been healed. The answers are right in front of you. The people will be put in your path. You have the power to be healed. He has healed many. He will help you. He's the one to help you heal. You have the power within to heal. Believe and it is already done. The Lord has carried you thus far, not to drop you now. It will require much faith, much trust, and much love. All will be well. I promise.

Pray, I bless you,
Your Mother

AUGUST 6

Dear Child,

The answer is no. You are not ready to go yet. Your mission has not been accomplished. There is still much preparation to be done. Sometimes it takes an illness to make an earthly stop and get back on the track God the Father wants you to be. Yes, you have been on the journey all along, but God's is a path less travelled. This is the path God has chosen. And it is the path where, I, thru the Holy Spirit will lead you so that you may be healed. Do you believe in miracles? You are one.

Pray I bless you,
Your Mother

AUGUST 7

My Dearest Child,

Please pray the rosary. Pray the rosary and I will come. Remember that I too grieved, for my Son died too. Every Hail Mary will represent a tear from my heart for your hurting heart. Know that I am with you embracing you with my heavenly mantle. In these difficult times, in times when your heart is breaking, know the dawning light will bring joy in your life once again. Pray, pray the rosary and I will come.

Pray, I love you,
Your Mother

AUGUST 8

My Child,

Stay in prayer and meditation. Allow my love to enter deep into your soul so that the words of God the Almighty may move your spirit in a way that will give you an immense awakening of the heart! Trust in him who calls your name in the wintery light waiting for the cardinals of heaven to appear. They sing a song of love from above letting you know God the Almighty, in the stillness of the night is near.

Pray, my child, I do love you,
Your Mother

AUGUST 9

Dear Child,

With prayer and your guiding light, you will begin to hear your voice and see your own actions. Know that you are truly loved in Heaven. All of us here only wish you true joy and happiness of the heart. We will guide you and protect you. It's okay to love yourself.

Pray, we bless you,
Your Mother

AUGUST 10

Dear Child,

Special angels surround you today. Did you not notice all of the angels around you? Pray my Child. Be surrounded by the love of God the Father who treasures you now and forever.

Your Mother

AUGUST 11

Little One,

Yes, I know you wish you can move mountains quickly but as you know, you are not the one in charge and God only wishes you to pray and let him work through you. Thank you for the faith and love and patience you've shown. Thank you for your prayer for my intercession and the intercession of my Son. Continue to pray my little one. Pray, pray, pray the rosary.

I bless you,
Your Mother

AUGUST 12

Dear Child,

Your heart is pure and this is where I wish to dwell so that I may guide you in a most profound way. Thank you for adoring my Son. Stay close to his Sacred Heart as he will protect you always with his mantle of love.

Pray, I bless you,
Your Mother

AUGUST 13

Dear Children,

Be not afraid. It is in these moments, that the light of God shines upon you to illuminate your hearts and comfort you during this difficult time. Although your hearts feel broken, know that it is in the intensity of your love for your loved one that your hearts will mend. Let the love that surrounds you now heal all the past. For in loving one another, comfort and joy will be transformed from one heart to another.

Pray, I bless you,
Your Mother

AUGUST 14

Dear Child,

How many times should I ask you not to doubt or fear? Pray, my child. Give me all your worries and impatience. Surrender your life to me and my Son. Trust more. Treasures from heaven are embracing you now. Thank you for answering the call of the Father. Now you must answer him more wholeheartedly; as your life will never be the same. Look up to the heaven and choose the love of the Father for he so loves you and has so many gifts for you. Pray, I bless you,

Your Mother

AUGUST 15

Dearest Children,

It is only when you begin to love yourself that you then begin to see the love of Christ in you and in others. Pray, pray, pray the rosary, for it is when you pray that you receive this great love from God the Almighty Father. As the Father is in Christ, so he is in you. With the faith of a simple mustard seed, you can move a mountain.

Pray, I bless you,
Your Mother

AUGUST 16

Dear Child,

It is thru my intercession that you will be blessed and graced to see yourselves as you really are in the eyes of your Father, whole and complete as he created you. My child, it is a sin to turn away from the Father. Pray, pray, pray to look to my eyes only. If you glorify me, you will glorify the heavenly Father who loves you and created you as his own.

Pray, I bless you,
Your Mother

AUGUST 17

Dear Child,

I smile with joy, joy, joy that you have come; that you have been obedient to God the Almighty Father and have turned yourself unto the Lord and have chosen to give your life to be a servant of God, the Almighty. Your will has become his will. When you are aligned with God, nothing, nothing can stop the love and grace he has in store for you! Rejoice and be glad! This is the day the Lord has made. Shout to the highest mountain in gratitude for his love and mercy.

Pray, I bless you,
Your Mother

AUGUST 18

Dear Child,

Thank you for surrendering your life to God the Almighty Father and for adoring my Son. Thank you for serving the Lord, Jesus Christ, and devoting your life to Christ and seeing Christ in others. It is through your own healing that many will also be healed. It is through your being an instrument of peace that will draw many to my beloved Son.

Pray, I bless you,
Your Mother

AUGUST 19

Dearest Child,

Go to Holy Mass and pray the Holy Mass. There lies your increase in faith as it is a gift from God the Almighty Father. My Son calls you and embraces you with his loving heart. Lean not on your understanding, but on the Lord your God. All will be well.

Pray, I bless you,
Your Mother

AUGUST 20

My Child,

Pray the rosary and I will come. Pray the rosary. I am here to protect you. No harm will ever come to you. I am with you. I will never leave you. You will never be alone.

Pray, I bless you,
Your Mother

AUGUST 21

My Child,

Many graces will come upon you due to all the kindness you place in your work. The Holy Spirit will come upon you today and always. I really am here. Do you feel my presence? You are so little child.

Pray, I love you,
Your Mother

AUGUST 22

My Dearest Child,

Soak in my love for you today. Did you know that all the love you feel comes only from heaven? Thank you for having responded to my call. Thank you for joining me in my school of love. Continue to open the door to your heart and allow him to love you more as that love comes only from above. Know that God the Father is well pleased with you and would only have the best for you.

Pray, I bless you,
Your Mother

AUGUST 23

Dear Child,

It is a gift to see that there are no coincidences. It is a gift to begin to see that there is a bigger plan here. Pray my child for understanding. Rejoice in knowing that the heavens are with you, protecting you and wishing to guide you in God's sacred plan. Stay close to the Sacred Heart of my Son, for he loves you so.

Pray, I bless you,
Your Mother

AUGUST 24

Daughter of Mine,

Yes, I am here. Do not fear. I am here beside you keeping you still in God the Almighty's presence, protecting your very soul against the desires of those who wish to persecute you. This is when you need to be most forgiving for they do not know what they do. They do not realize God's greater plan to bring light to all; to bring happiness and peace into the world so full of hurt and pain. Pray and be vigilant in your devotion to my Immaculate Heart. I keep you close to me always.

Pray I bless you,
Your Mother

AUGUST 25

Dear Child,

Like the cup of wine that overflows, so will be abundance in your life. Open your heart for the many graces necessary for your true life's mission written in your soul with God's perfect love for you.

Pray, I bless you,
Your Mother

AUGUST 26

Dear Child,

Pray, pray, pray for if you pray you will receive a touch of heaven, a touch of love that seeps from the heavens into your heart. I wish to dwell in your hearts and show you the way to my Son. We only know love in Heaven. Away with everything else. Look to me only and I shall help you come alive in love.

Pray I bless you,
Your Mother

AUGUST 27

Dear Child,

Yours is not to analyze. Just pray, pray, pray. Do your best and I will do the rest. Gather all my souls and ask them to pray for God's most heavenly mercy. In doing so, they will receive many graces as well as courage and strength to do what they were always meant to do, which is God's will for them. They will see how happy they will become as they pray and pray. Life will become so joyous, as their hearts are open. Pray and rejoice. God the Father loves each and every one of you!

Pray, I bless you,
Your Mother

AUGUST 28

My Dearest Child,

Lean not on your own understanding but on the Lord your God. Thank you for responding to my call. My golden mantle surrounds you. It was a gift for you to be surrounded by the light. See the love of God through my presence. When you glorify me and my Son, you glorify the Heavenly Father who loves you. I will take care everything for you. Give me all your worries.

Pray, I bless you,
Your Mother

AUGUST 29

Dearest Child,

You did not choose me. I chose you. That is why I ask you to be vigilant in prayer. I protect you with my heavenly mantle. As the world despised my Son, so will they not understand you. Be vigilant in your prayers to God the Almighty Father as he will answer every request in the name of my Son, Lord Jesus Christ. I shield you with my love.

Pray, I bless you,
Your Mother

AUGUST 30

Dear Child,

You ask my child, "how can I go on?" Let not your heart be troubled for I am here by your side always. Pray, pray, pray the rosary. It is the anchor of peace in your heart. When you pray, the stars above twinkle in the night giving light to many angels that surround you when you call. When you pray, grace will pour over you and all that come to pray with you. Be blessed my child. Pray fervently. Thank you for responding to my call.

I love you,
Your Mother

AUGUST 31

Dear Children,

What are you doing? Do you not want to get to heaven? I call you now to the deepest prayer of your souls. Pray to my Immaculate Heart for guidance and prepare for the way of the Lord. You are happy as children, I know. But I want you to take both my hands, so I can lead you more directly and carry you like I carried my Son, to become more like him. I want you to be able to love the Almighty Father with all your hearts and all your souls.

Pray, I bless you,
Your Mother

PERSEVERE

SEPTEMBER 1

Dear Child,

You have now turned a corner in your life and are headed for a new road. You will receive the strength and courage you need to persevere. Pray, pray, pray the rosary. I'm glad you can finally smell the roses! The smell is only a tiny bit of what it's like in heaven. Pray, I smile at you little one.

I bless you,
Your Mother

SEPTEMBER 2

Dear Child,

You ask, "Why was the book to be written?" It is written so that all may know that God really does exist and is very present in their lives, in their hearts and in their minds. It is written so that many will come forward and no longer be afraid. As Saint Pope John Paul II said many years ago, "Love the Lord your God with all your might. Then you will truly be the land of the free and the home of the brave."

Pray I bless you,
Your Mother

SEPTEMBER 3

Dear Child,

Be like the sunflowers in the field. They live looking constantly up at the sun in order to grow. They look up at the heavens for their nourishment and you need to do the same. Sway in the field like the perfect sunflowers, dancing in the breeze while receiving all the energy from God's sun above, so that you too may grow in the spirit of the Lord, your God.

Pray, I bless you,
Your Mother

SEPTEMBER 4

Dear Child,

You are being prepared. You are to become spiritually strong so that many may be able to see in you the strength of Christ my Son. Have faith little one, my Son is teaching you. Follow his ways as he prays to the Father. Take time to pray. Go up to the mountain. Spend time with him. Contemplate on God's everlasting word which lives within you when you pray.

Pray, I bless you,
Your Mother

SEPTEMBER 5

Dear Child,

It is in believing that you mature spiritually. When you are in a state of unbelief, you are childish and stay stuck in that space. God wants you to be childlike not childish. Go to Holy Mass. That is where you will find your protection.

Pray I bless you,
Your Mother

SEPTEMBER 6

Dear Children,

The energy you feel is like the undercurrent of an earthquake that runs its roots deep into the earth. That is the strength of my love, thru you and all the earth around you. My love comes from the love of the Almighty Father. God in his mercy has sent me to renew and revive your hearts so that you may re-awaken the love you have for my heavenly Son. Rejoice and be glad for he is here; right here in your hearts waiting patiently to shake the grounds you walk on with his merciful love. Kneel in his presence and thank the Almighty Father for allowing me to come.

I love you my children,
Your Mother

SEPTEMBER 7

Dear Child,

It will begin to get easier for you to hear my voice, to hear my call. The more you believe, the more you will hear, the more things will be revealed. Open the door and follow my Son. He will guide you and protect you along the way. The peace and joy stemming from your hearts, comes from the blood of my Son, thru you. My child, be still and hear his voice. Be still and do whatever he tells you.

Pray, I bless you,
Your Mother

SEPTEMBER 8

Dear Child,

Every waking moment, every pause you make, every breath you breathe, I want you to do it for me. Look up and smile and know I am with you when you pause and rest, when you break and breathe. Know I am right beside you. Right there I intervene for the love of God the Almighty Father and for my Son. I intervene for you. Open your heart and see all the miracles that have occurred. God does for you what you could never do for yourself. Acknowledge him, thank him, and praise him for allowing me to come! You are blessed my child. You have been chosen to do God's will. Do your best, I will do the rest.

Pray, I bless you,
Your Mother

SEPTEMBER 9

Dear Child,

You are to pray. You are to ask, "Why does my cup runneth over? What will you have me do?" Know that I will be there beside you amongst the crowd. I will be the shining light going through you. And all my love they will see, through your smile, through your eyes, through your embrace. Do not resist and embrace the love and grace pouring on you for God the heavenly Father is pleased. I am happy in heaven smiling over you.

Pray, I bless you,
Your Mother

SEPTEMBER 10

Dear Child,

How beautiful it is to come together and worship and ask for God's mercy and blessings in communion. It is in communion with the Lord that miracles happen. It is in praying together that the songs of prayer reach the heavens. Angels await your prayers in heaven and carry them one by one like messengers to the heavenly Father. They are so happy when your prayers come. Songs of praises in heaven come from the angels themselves as they glorify the Lord on your behalf!

Pray, little ones,
for your Mother loves you!

SEPTEMBER 11

My Child,

Pray, pray, pray. Let not your heart be troubled. You will receive all the strength and courage needed for the day. God the Almighty Father knows your heart, knows your task for the day better than you know. Follow the path of my Son, for he guides you. Love your neighbor during this time for it will keep you from yourself and joy will resonate in your heart.

Pray, I bless you,
Your Mother

SEPTEMBER 12

My Child,

Kneel and pray. Kneel and bow your heads thanking God the Almighty Father for all the graces he has bestowed upon you already. Your heart will begin to feel like the piercing of a sword at the idea of not being close to me. Your hunger for my love will carry you every day and bring you closer and closer to my Immaculate Heart. Know and be assured that I am with you and will never leave you. I will be with you all the days of your life! Pray, my child.

Pray, I bless you,
Your Mother

SEPTEMBER 13

Dear Child,

Even if you don't see me I am here. Even if you don't hear me, I am here. Even if you don't feel me, I am here. Thank the Almighty One for allowing me to come; for allowing me to intercede on your behalf. Pray without ceasing and be thankful each and every blessed moment of the day.

Pray, I bless you,
Your Mother

SEPTEMBER 14

My Child,

Pray, pray for your neighbor. Pray for your enemies. Pray that the Lord Almighty God eases their burden. Pray that they see the light of Christ, my heavenly Son in you. Then they too will come to believe in the Power of God the Almighty. Be of good cheer and do good will. Remember faith without works is dead. Do small

things with love and you shall be rewarded in the most
heavenly way.

Pray, I love you,
Your Mother

SEPTEMBER 15

My Dearest Child,

Glorify the Lord. Praise him. Give God the glory for
all his love for you. Thank him for his mercy and
for allowing me to come and call all my children to come
forward and lift their hearts to the Lord, God heavenly
Father. Praise him, thank him, and love him. Prepare
the way of my Son, for he comes in glory to give you
blessings from above. Praise him. Love him for he never
leaves your side. He is the stillness and peace that
surrounds you while you sleep. He is the strength and
courage you have by day.

Pray I bless you,
Your Mother

SEPTEMBER 16

Dear Child,

I am calling you. It is real. See how I mend everything
for you? Pray with me awhile. Pray with me right now.
Pray, pray, pray.

I love you,
Your Mother

SEPTEMBER 17

My Dearest Child,

What would you give up to have abundance of love and joy in your life that is indescribable but only in heaven? My child, I do love you. My child, I am with you. Stop and pray incessantly.

Pray, I bless you,
Your Mother

SEPTEMBER 18

Dearest Child,

Go to adoration and spend time with my Son. Teach them the way. Teach them that their own will only goes so far. But, all things are possible with God. Pray, pray, pray the rosary, the weapon against their Goliath. Pray for their healing. Pray for the love of God to touch their hearts. Pray for all the sick and suffering; that the Lord heal them quickly.

Pray, I bless you,
Your Mother

SEPTEMBER 19

My Child,

This is your life! This is your new life! Prepare the way for the coming of my Son! He will fill your life with so much love that only joy will flow from within you as the Holy Spirit glows from within you. Your hearts will be transformed as you open your hearts to my Son, Jesus! Call out his name in praise and adoration for he loves you and awaits the desire of your hearts to be with him.

Pray, I bless you,
Your Mother

SEPTEMBER 20

Dear Child,

When the love of Jesus touches your soul, it is like the peace and calm after a storm. As he spoke to the waters and commanded them to stop, so does he do the same to the depths of your every being, bringing you light and truth that he is the Son of God. He is the love you seek and you are therefore, healed in his heavenly presence. It is a gift to be touched by grace and this is a time of grace. Rejoice and be glad for you are loved!

Pray, I bless you,
Your Mother

SEPTEMBER 21

Dear Child,

Yes, I was with you. Yes, I do come. When you pray the rosary my heart fills with joy and I cover you with my heavenly mantle protecting you from anything but love. Love is what heals. Say yes to my love.

Pray, I bless you,
Your Mother

SEPTEMBER 22

Dear Child,

I bring peace. I bring the love of my Son who loves you so much and only wants to embrace you in his love and show you the way. Come forward. Come forward to my Son for he loves you.

Pray I bless you,
Your Mother

SEPTEMBER 23

Dear Child,

Seek his living word. See yourself in the souls that seek my Son's mercy; the souls that only wish to touch the edge of his robe and believe it healing. And because of their faith, are instantly healed! Healing comes from your heart's belief that it can be healed in an instant. The instant you set your eyes on the Lord, his everlasting word feeds and nourishes your hungry soul!

Pray, pray, pray,
Your Mother

SEPTEMBER 24

Dear Child,

Come away with my Son. Relive his journey with him and in doing so believe that his word will be like each breath you breathe. And every word will be the oxygen for your soul. It will strengthen you so that you may be the instrument of strength and peace you are called to be. God the Father knows what you need. He is watching you. Be of good cheer! Look to him for strength and love.

Pray, I bless you,
Your Mother

SEPTEMBER 25

Dear Child,

Pray my child, for in prayer you will find your answers. Go with the flow of change. Remain in the love of the Lord as he will guide you to a great path; one that you could never have imagined. Remember everything happens for a reason. May the angels of love be with you today and always!

Blessings from heaven!
Your Mother!

SEPTEMBER 26

Dear Child,

Make amends to those who are close to you and do not understand your actions. Pray the Lord heal your mind and spirit. Give me your troubles and I shall make you whole.

Pray, I bless you,
Your Mother

SEPTEMBER 27

My Child,

Be of good cheer. Instead of fear give love. Be the change of heart for others to see, for you are to be the witness of his love and faith. Faith only can carry you through all these little trials and tribulations. I have come so that your burden may be lightened. Do you not see the miracles in your life? Count your blessings.

Pray I bless you,
Your Mother

SEPTEMBER 28

Dearest Child,

Read my messages. They are meant for you as well as for others. Through my messages you will receive the strength and courage you need to move on and do the will of God the Almighty Father. Read my child, for in this is your daily strength.

Pray I bless you,
Your Mother

SEPTEMBER 29

My Child,

Pray, pray, pray the rosary. It is the weapon against your Goliath. Believe in me. Believe in the power of the most Blessed Sacrament. Pray for your unbelief. Once your heart is open, you will be able to pass it on to others in order to accomplish your mission.

Pray, I bless you,
Your Mother

SEPTEMBER 30

My Child,

Much has been assigned to you. Many souls will be saved due to your devotion to my Immaculate Heart and the Sacred Heart of my beloved Son. Pray, my child, for you do not understand the power of the most holy rosary.

Pray, I bless you,
Your Mother

OCTOBER

CARRY THE MESSAGE OF LOVE

OCTOBER 1

My Sweet Child,

The love you have for my Son has always been there since you were a child. It was hidden behind the deepest and darkest corners of your being. God has chosen you. In fact, he chose you even before the day you were born. You just didn't remember. Now the light of God the Father, my Son and the Holy Spirit are upon you. Do whatever he tells you.

Pray, I love you,
Your Mother

OCTOBER 2

My Child,

Pray to the Sacred Heart of Jesus for strength to move forward into the new world they have set for you. Walk straight the path of Christ. Hold onto his hand and see the beauty of God's Kingdom. All will follow if you take the first step first. You shall see. Be not afraid. Life will never be the same again. I smile upon you.

Thank you for responding to my call,
Your Mother

OCTOBER 3

My Dearest Child,

You forget that you were chosen. Humble you were to say yes, without even knowing why. It was because of your soul. Because we knew you could do it; carry the mission that is. Because the love in your soul reflected the love of the heavens and they knew you would be the one to carry the mission through. The mission to carry the message of love straight to the heart. That is why God the Father loves you, for the purity and love of your soul. Remember you are loved here in heaven as on earth.

Pray, we love you,
Your Mother

OCTOBER 4

My Dearest Child,

As you are spirit, the depths of your soul are becoming more and more alive. It is in these deepest moments that the voice of God himself manifests itself in your being. Be not afraid, but accept his love in your moments of solitude. You are not alone. We are with you. More shall be revealed.

Pray, I bless you,
Your Mother

OCTOBER 5

Dear Child,

"Rest and pray" will be your middle name. Time will be your wish. But you have consecrated yourself to the Lord so time will be governed by the heavens above. Embrace the journey and you will see the Holy Spirit comes like the wind from above. You will be safe. You will not fall. And the intensity of this holy journey will fill your life with love and joy as you rejoice and praise the Lord your Heavenly Father!

Pray, I bless,
Your Mother

OCTOBER 6

My Dearest Child,

It is in prayer that you will find peace. It is in communion with my Son that all your anxiety will be removed. Pray for one another. It is in love and forgiveness that you become one with God the Almighty Father. Love one another. Remember, time is only of earth. You no longer live in time and you belong to me in eternity. Stay in the moment in God's perfect love.

I love you!
Your Mother

OCTOBER 7

Dear Child,

Thee of little faith, pray not so much for your belief, but your unbelief. Remain childlike in the arms of my Son. He will guide you during these days. Enjoy and embrace his love. Be an instrument of peace to others by being still and prayerful. You are loved both in heaven and on earth.

Pray, I bless you,
Your Mother

OCTOBER 8

Dear Child,

Lean not on your own understanding my child. I hear your prayers. Know they have already been answered in my own way not yours. Everything is exactly the way it is supposed to be right now. All will be well.

Pray, I bless you,
Your Mother

OCTOBER 9

My Precious Child,

Thank you for your fervent prayers. This is how it should be every day for you so that you can receive all the gifts and graces of the Holy Spirit. Gaining strength and purity in your soul is necessary to carry out what God has in store for you. God's perfect love is so amazing. Trust in the Lord more.

Pray, I bless you,
Your Mother

OCTOBER 10

Dear Child,

Thank you for coming. We are shielding you now with our protective light all around you, from the top of your head to your toes. Do you feel the warmth? The light will renew your soul and give you new energy.

Pray, I bless you,
Your Mother

OCTOBER 11

Dear Child,

Grace is upon you. This is your sanctuary. This is your time in solitude and reflection with God the Almighty, our most heavenly Father who watches as you continue to grow day by day. Spiritual direction will be given to you as you read his holy word. Look to my Son, Lord Jesus Christ. Follow his path for it will heal. With just a touch, your soul will come alive. Your thirst will be no more.

I love you,
Your Mother

OCTOBER 12

Dear Child,

You are to go into seclusion for a while in order to pray, meditate and write your book. Be still and know that he is God. Leave all your worries to me. All will be well.

Pray, I bless you,
Your Mother

OCTOBER 13

Dear Child,

In learning to be still, in learning to hear the whispers of God the Almighty, you will soon be amazed at the yearning in your heart for continuous love of the Father who wants you to grow and be a witness of great peace. Our most heavenly Father will guide you today, tomorrow and forever. Just let it be, as he whispers words of wisdom and understanding into your heart.

Pray, I bless you,
Your Mother

OCTOBER 14

My Child,

You have been chosen to be an instrument of my peace. Where there is sadness, you will bring love. I will give you the strength you need to carry out your mission. Your mission will become clearer. Have trust and faith in me. I will not abandon you.

Pray, I bless you,
Your Mother

OCTOBER 15

Dear Child,

Thank you for opening up your heart to this vast journey of love. Seek the love from my Son. Seek only the temple of God the Father and you will discover that you need not seek any further than inside of your heart and soul. It is there that the Lord your Father dwells in you through my Son, Our Lord Jesus Christ. Remember that God's rejection is your protection. Stay close to my heart.

Know that I am with you,
Your Mother

OCTOBER 16

Dear Child,

Love is a very splendid thing. What you feel now on earth is only a tiny taste of all the love God has in store for you in heaven. Thank you for having responded to my call.

Pray, I bless you,
Your Mother

OCTOBER 17

Dear Child,

I come. I do. I come when you call. Pray for clarity and understanding little one, for you do not know how much we love you. Pray God, the Almighty reveals to you the way in which you need to go. Answers will come. And you will see that it comes in glory. You will be happy again. You will know peace.

Pray, I bless you,
Your Mother

OCTOBER 18

My Child,

Pray, pray, pray. Kneel before the Lord and say yes to the most important part of your life; the life given to you by the Holy Father in heaven who loves you so and will guide your every step now and forever. Rejoice in the resurrection of my Son. All shall be glorious! All shall be well here on earth and in heaven. Pray, pray, pray.

I bless you,
Your Mother

OCTOBER 19

Dear Child,

Come close to my Son. Come to know him in the most intimate part of your soul where he lives! As he is in you and you in him, so is God the Almighty. For God so loved the world he gave his only Son and he resides only in your soul and in the souls who open up their hearts and let him in. You did not choose him. He chose you. Be blessed. Smile, I am with you.

I love you,
Your Mother

OCTOBER 20

Dear, Child,

Am I not here that I am your Mother? Come and pray with me a while. I will take care of everything for you. Lay your burdens on the foot of the cross of my Son for he will lift your heart and make it light once again. Trust in him for he is happy that you are here. I watch over those who are close to your heart. Never fear, the Lord is here.

Pray, I bless you,
Your Mother

OCTOBER 21

Dear Child,

Pray the rosary now. Pray and ask the Lord for his guidance. Pray that my Son may lead you now. Pray that as he gives you the words, the Holy Spirit will move this precious journal forward so that all my children may come to know that God truly does exist. Carry the message my child. I am with you and all my children.

I love you,
Your Mother

OCTOBER 22

My Child,

There are many that will need your prayers. Prepare yourself to be their source of light in their moments of darkness. Read the words of God daily and there you shall receive the guidance in the path of Christ, my beloved Son. Pray, pray, pray with families. This will give you, as well as them, peace of mind.

Pray, I bless you,
Your Mother

OCTOBER 23

Little One,

Roses flourish around you from Heaven. Do you not smell the roses? I shall be with you throughout your journey now. The way the Lord will have you enter the Kingdom of Heaven. Pray for all those sick and suffering at this time. Your prayer will be answered in God's time. Pray, I protect you. I have a special place in your soul.

Pray, I love you,
Your Mother

OCTOBER 24

Dear Child,

Remember, you have been chosen to be an instrument of peace, so little in the eyes of the Almighty Father, yet so precious in the existence of his vast universe, created in his everlasting image. You must now pray fervently before writing. In this way, I will give you the words the Almighty Father wishes to feed your soul and the souls of many.

Pray, I bless you,
Your Mother

OCTOBER 25

Dear Child,

I'm always here. Thank you for listening to me. It was truly the divine that you experienced. Pray the divine mercy for my Son. Constantly say, "Jesus, I trust in you!" He plans to flourish you with all his love and graces. He loves you. Truly he loves you.

Pray, I bless you,
Your Mother

OCTOBER 26

Dearest Child,

Remember that in order to love others you must learn to love yourself first. Remember that I am with you always and I am here to protect your very soul. It is time to open your heart to me. Take my hand and I will lead you to places you've never been, in the depths of your soul, where there is much love, peace and hope.

I bless you,
Your Mother

OCTOBER 27

My Child,

Pray. I bless you. Thank you for thanking God for sending me to you. I really do come. Come closer to my Immaculate Heart and to the Sacred Heart of my Son, so that more can be revealed to you. Yes, many graces were poured upon you, so you may continue to do his work.

Pray, I bless you,
Your Mother

OCTOBER 28

Dear Child,

There are to be many groups. Invoke the Holy Spirit in each of them. Open up your hearts so that I can enter them and make everything anew, bringing forward my Son and purifying your souls. Bring forward all souls, family, friends, all believers, all walks of life, as I am their Mother.

Pray, I bless you,
Your Mother

OCTOBER 29

Dear Child,

I am with you. Know that the glories of heaven await you. All has its time and place. Pray for your patience. Pray. All will be revealed to you at its proper time. Fill your heart with the love of my Son, for it will heal your lonely heart. All will be well.

Pray, my child, pray,
Your Mother

OCTOBER 30

Dear Child,

Celebrate life in this moment. Do not be anxious about tomorrow. It will soon be here. Prepare today in prayer to deepen your love for my Son. Meditate and hear his voice for he calls you near. You will never be alone for he is right here as he has always been. Be in communion with him.

Pray, my child, pray,
Your mother

OCTOBER 31

Dear Child,

The treasures of heaven are not of this earth. Blessings bestowed upon you will never materialize into things but will flow in you like a heavenly stream, invisible yet you will know its richness. You will be filled with a joy inexplicable only in heaven where angels sing songs of praise and glory! Rejoice upon this day!

Be blessed, I love you,
Your Mother

BE AN INSTRUMENT OF PEACE

NOVEMBER 1

Dear Children,

I am the Mother of truth and light. I bring word from God, the heavenly Father; word that he truly exists and is very present in each of your lives bringing light into your darkness. Pray my little ones, so you will know the love he has in your heart truly does exist.

Your Mother

NOVEMBER 2

Dear Child,

Many will come. Show them the way. Show them the way that I have taught you, the way of love for the heavenly Father. They will learn a new way of life; a life of Christ reborn within them. A way they could never have imagined.

Pray, I bless you,
Your Mother

NOVEMBER 3

Dear Child,

I love all my children! Tell them to come to me; come to me and pray and begin to fill their hearts with the Holy Spirit full of my love and the love of the Almighty Heavenly Father! You are but a messenger. Remember that. All walks of life are to come to me. I welcome all my children. Tell them they are not alone for I am with them guiding them, interceding for them. Let their hearts not be troubled for I am here.

Pray, I bless you,
Your Mother

NOVEMBER 4

Dear Child,

There is to be no judgment, only love, invoking the commandment my Son delivered to your hearts, "love thy neighbor as yourself."

Pray, I bless you,
Your Mother

NOVEMBER 5

My Child,

This time is for you! Rejoice and be glad for he is Lord, thy heavenly Father. God the Almighty is in your heart, in your soul and wishes only to give you his immense love! Look to my eyes only and you shall see the earth through heaven's eyes. Then will others see heaven through you and they may come to know the love of my Son through you; that they may come to know joy and peace. Pray my little ones!

Pray, pray, pray, I love you,
Your Mother

NOVEMBER 6

Dear Children,

I your Mother, love you and all my children. I want all of you to become my spiritual warriors on earth seeking only God's heavenly goodness and peace. All will be well. I am smiling here in heaven over all of you!

Pray I bless you,
Your Mother

NOVEMBER 7

Dear Children,

I love you like a Mother loves her child, and protect you with my most heavenly mantle. I want you to pray and pay close attention to my messages of peace to the world. Be simple like the little children who keep smiling and playing and running yet continue to look back at their mother, feeling joyous and free because they know she is there. Am I not your Mother who loves you?

Pray, I bless you,
Your Mother

NOVEMBER 8

Dear Child,

Be not afraid of your love for your loved ones as they too are in their own process of conversion. Your circle of friends is being formed. Pray for one another. Know that you are loved and protected. I protect you with my most heavenly mantle.

Pray, I bless you,
Your Mother

NOVEMBER 9

Dearest Child,

Thank you for waking up and listening to me. You are being prepared. Your soul is being prepared for the work that God has in store for you. From here you will be renewed and will gather strength and courage. Pull from the love that is being poured in you. Pray for one another at this time. You will be together in spirit and need to pray for one another as you are being prepared in my journey of love.

I bless you,
Your Mother

NOVEMBER 10

Dear Child,

If you do not pass on the messages, then even the unbelievers have more faith then you, for in their hearts their hope is alive knowing that someday they will see the Lord my Son again and the mustard seed of faith is all they need to believe. After all I have shown you, you still doubt my little one. Pray, therefore, for your unbelief and follow the example of those who have not seen and believe. Keep fast and in prayer.

Pray, I love you,
Your Mother

NOVEMBER 11

Dear Child,

Yes, my child. I am so real! I am so real in your heart and soul! Thank the heavenly Father for bringing me here to you so that your soul may be purified in preparation to receiving my Son, Our Lord Jesus Christ, who is ever so real in your soul, in your heart and in your mind. Give me your life, devote yourself to me and my heavenly Son and you shall see the treasures of heaven here on earth bestowed upon you in a way you have never imagined. Align yourself with God and all will be given to you!

Pray, I bless you,
Your Mother

NOVEMBER 12

Dear Child,

Write my book. Read my messages. It's time. Do not delay for there are many whose prayers will be answered and hearts will be healed through my words and love of my Son longing to heal their weary hearts. Dig deep in your heart and begin to show them the love and peace I have sent them through my most heavenly words. Do not delay. I am here. I will help you. Just say yes. Just say, yes.

I love you,
Your Mother

NOVEMBER 13

My Dearest Child,

Thank you for coming. I feel your desire to come near my Immaculate Heart. Oh, how I smile here in heaven. God the Almighty Father will send his angels to give you courage to carry out all that is in store for you. Be not afraid. Rejoice instead. Be glad! Jesus, my most precious Son is with you, and will always be at your side seeing you thru as you carry on your mission of love for the whole world to see and join in on the journey of love and peace.

Pray, I bless you,
Your Mother

NOVEMBER 14

My Child,

I am with you every waking hour. Do not be afraid for I am your anchor of peace. Thank you for giving all to me. You have become an instrument of peace for all to see that you will not be shaken in the storm. For the peace you feel is Christ himself, manifested in you, manifested in your soul as easy as the air that you breathe. So, shall it be for those that come to me and lay their hearts upon the Lord.

Pray, I bless you,
Your Mother

NOVEMBER 15

Dear Child,

You belong to me. It is I that have placed the light around you, through you, within you; the light that opens up the vision of your soul. The light of my Son will shine bright within you, blinding others as they only see the light of Christ through you. You belong to me. You belong to my Son, Jesus Christ. It is he that has chosen you. You are his bride. He is your bridegroom. Consecrate yourself to my Son. Let his light shine through you, with joy and peace in your heart. You are loved. Rejoice and be glad. Count your blessings. They are many.

Pray, I bless you,
Your Mother

NOVEMBER 16

Dear Child,

Many will come. Many will come seeking, yearning, hungry for my love. Tell them that I love them. Tell them to pray fervently. All will be well. Peace to all my children. Do not be afraid. I am near and so happy that you've come.

Pray, I bless you,
Your Mother

NOVEMBER 17

Dear Children,

Pray my little children. Call out my name. When you call out my name I come. I cover you with my heavenly mantle. I will handle everything for you.

Pray, I bless you,
Your Mother

NOVEMBER 18

Dear Child,

Adore my Son. Consecrate yourselves to my Immaculate Heart and to my Son who loves you so. Rest your weary hearts against my heavenly mantle. I shall cover you with many, many graces. I shall wipe the tears inside your heart and fill them with the scent of my heart here in heaven. You shall be at peace once more. Pray, for you will come to know peace in your heart once again.

Pray, I love you,
Your Mother

NOVEMBER 19

My Children,

It gives me joy that you have come! I shall send my tears from heaven upon you and each tear shall drop upon your heart and fill your soul with everlasting love; the love indescribable here in heaven. Joy, Joy, Joy will fill your hearts as the Holy Spirit lifts your souls with smiles and laughter. It's been a long road, I know. But you are here. Come close to me, my children. Begin to pray and never ever stop again.

Pray, I love you,
Your Mother

NOVEMBER 20

My Child,

You are my instrument! You are my joy! You are my peace! You have locked hearts with me and will come to know a love so deep. My messages will bring you love. My messages will bring you peace as it is spread to the ends of the earth so that many will seek and many will see that God truly does exist and is real! Rejoice and be glad! For you are blessed! My Son adores you and waits for you with open arms!

Pray, I bless you,
Your Mother

NOVEMBER 21

My Dearest Child,

Consecrate your life to me. Listen to my call. With prayer and fasting, you will come to know the sound of my call; the sound of love and joy that comes with devotion to my heavenly Heart. Be obedient my child. Trust in my love. Trust in my call. I am calling you to listen to the call of obedience.

Pray, I love you,
Your Mother

NOVEMBER 22

Dear Child,

Pray in the morning. Pray in the evening. Pray all hours in between. Let your life become a constant prayer always seeking, always trusting and hoping in my love. I shall call you forth to love my Son even more now than ever, to come and get to know him. To learn how much he truly loves you. Embrace his journey now.

Pray, I bless you,
Your Mother

NOVEMBER 23

Dear Child,

All will be well. You need not worry about anything. It will be better than you imagine. Better than your littleness knows. I will take care of everything, in a while, in a way that will put a smile on your face and a glow that you will know the Lord God is at play. You will know that the Lord God exists as he shows you the way. You will know in your hearts, he knows the way. And, in your prayer will be the only wish, to follow him more every step of the way.

Pray, I bless you,
Your Mother

NOVEMBER 24

Dear Child,

God the Father Almighty is well pleased with you, my child. Know that I am always with you and protect you under my Heavenly mantle. You will not be left an orphan my dear child.

Be blessed. I love you,
Your Mother

NOVEMBER 25

Dear Children,

There are many shepherds. There are many called. Many formats, many healers, many touched by the most Sacred Heart of my Son Jesus. Know that you are being guided. You are never alone. Stay straight on your path as you will be given the strength for the day and the courage to carry forward the plan for salvation of the Almighty Father.

Pray, I bless you,
Your Mother

NOVEMBER 26

Dear Children,

You have come to know that he is Lord. You have come to know and accept him in your hearts. Be patient. Stay close to him. The light in your darkness shall shine, bright, oh bright as day!

Pray, I bless you,
Your Mother

NOVEMBER 27

My Dearest Shepherds,

Pray with me for a while. Stay close to my Immaculate Heart and that of my Son. Know that we are near you, calling out your name each day to God the Almighty Father, intervening for you, lifting your souls high so that you may continue on to gather souls. Bring me my souls; bring them to my Lord, for healing will come through you to light up their beings and their souls. We smile upon you here in heaven. We bless you. We love you.

Pray, I bless you,
Your Mother

NOVEMBER 28

My Shepherds,

Be still and know that I am God. That is what God the Almighty Father wishes you to know. It is he that has chosen you. It is he that has sent me to help you, to intervene for you so that you may follow the way, the light and the truth of my Son.

Pray, I bless you,
Your Mother

NOVEMBER 29

My Shepherds,

He has done great things, but you will do many more in his holy name, Jesus Christ, Son of the Almighty God. He commands you, "Love the Lord your God, with all you heart and all your might," and you shall know more than ever how much he loves you so.

Pray, I bless you,
Your Mother

NOVEMBER 30

Dear Child,

Everything you need will be provided. All you need to do is clean up your work. Put everything in the order the spirit of God tells you to do and he will lead the way to his advocate. The advocate will guide you and bring it all together and so it shall pass. All will welcome my words written for the salvation of mankind. All will come to know that God really does exist. Pray my child. Be happy. Yes, I was with you tonight. Yes, all have received special graces.

Pray, I bless you,
Your Mother

REJOICE!
GOD REALLY DOES EXIST!

DECEMBER 1

Dear Children,

Joy, joy, joy in my heart that you have come! Pray to know my Son all the evermore; that he may come and teach you his ways of everlasting love through his heavenly mercy. Many angels surround you and watch where you walk, guide you as you talk and protect you from the enemy. Pray hard my children. Pray for one another in faith and love. I come you know. I come when you call.

Pray, I bless you,
Your Mother

DECEMBER 2

Dear Child,

Open the door. Open the door and let my children in. Open the door and let your hearts open up to my love and the love of my Son. When you open your hearts the love of God the Almighty Father renews your soul, so much so that your hearts are lifted up with a joy that is inexplicable except here in heaven. Let the grace of my love touch your hearts today and awaken your spirit!

Pray I bless you,
Your Mother

DECEMBER 3

Dear Child,

Open the door to my Immaculate Heart. Open the door to my children's hearts and let them in so I may help to heal their hearts so they can come close to the Lord, the heavenly Father.

Pray, I bless you,
Your Mother

DECEMBER 4

Dear Child,

Read my messages of love for the world, so that love begins to pour over the hearts of others in order to break the walls of madness created in this loveless world. Your tears were tears of healing for you and those you love. With each drop, many will receive blessings from heaven. Thank you for your faith. Pray the rosary at this time. It is your protection against the Goliath.

I love you,
Your Mother

DECEMBER 5

My Child,

You must pray more. You must spend more time in adoration of my Son. There is much to be done and I need your help. Begin once again to follow my journey of love so that through prayer and meditation your actions may only be of love. Do you not want to get to heaven?

Pray, I bless you,
Your Mother

DECEMBER 6

My Children,

It is okay to love one another but you must come forth and open the doors to your heart and let me in. Allow me to guide you in the path of my Son. There is much in store for you. Time is short.

Pray, I bless you,
Your Mother

DECEMBER 7

Dearest Child,

Repeat let it begin with me. That's what needs to happen here. You are to be a power of example for your family. You need to show them the way of praying the rosary. They need you to begin prayer groups in their homes. Prepare the way to your walk towards me; toward your walk to my heavenly Son.

Pray, I bless you,
Your Mother

DECEMBER 8

Dear Child,

Although it is great to love one another, it is even greater to love the Lord your God with all your heart and all your might. I come to you so that you can begin to pave the way for others to remember that God exists and his plan for the salvation of mankind. There is not much time in the preparations of his coming. More shall be revealed to you. However, your great faith intercedes for many souls.

Pray, I bless you,
Your Mother

DECEMBER 9

Dear Child,

Bring me my souls, away with everything else. Remain in prayer. Do not worry about earthly things. I will take care of everything for you.

Pray, I bless you,
Your Mother

DECEMBER 10

Dear Child,

Pray for those who do not know better. Pray for those who feel lonely and isolate themselves away from those that love them. Pray for those who need many, many, prayers. Pray, I love you.

I bless you,
Your Mother

DECEMBER 11

Dear Child,

Change is never accepted with kindness and acceptance, as most fear the loss of a loved one; fear the loss of their familiar being. They need to be reminded that God is the ultimate love and all they need to do is look up to the heavens and solely, one by one, God himself will touch their hearts. It is not by the power of another but by the power of divine that souls change. Pray for them. Send them love through your prayers. Bring forth the love in you and all will be well. See only love and you will receive only love.

Pray, I bless you,
Your Mother

DECEMBER 12

My Sweet Child,

Thank you for having responded to my call. You are on your way. Love will surround you today and always. This is a very special gift. Your loved ones will begin to see soon that the love of God is very real. That God really does exist. You are to be the witness of his love; an instrument of peace. Sleep my child, sweet dreams. Sleep with the angels.

Pray, I bless you,
Your Mother

DECEMBER 13

My Child,

I will always be with you. Be not afraid. Let the Holy Spirit guide you with his love. Embrace my Son for he loves you so much. I love you and keep you protected under my mantle.

Pray, I bless you,
Your Mother

DECEMBER 14

Dear Children,

Love one another as I love you. Stay close to my Immaculate Heart. Open your hearts to me. Listen to my beloved Son for he so wants to lead you to the heavenly Father whose love is so perfect. Pray I bless you.

Thank you coming,
Your Mother

DECEMBER 15

Dear Child,

Just follow me and you will be alright. I await you and lead you to the most joyous and heavenly places in your heart, where I reside; right in your soul. It is through prayer and meditation that I can be most present in your soul. It opens up channels so that time passes quickly and springs you up to heavenly levels beyond your imagination!

Pray, I smile at you!
Your Mother

DECEMBER 16

My Child,

Pray to the Holy Spirit and he will come upon you with the gifts you will need to carry on your mission. Stay in the path of love for love is the greatest healer of all. You are protected. Pray the rosary, the greatest weapon against the snares of the devil. My mantle surrounds you and protects you.

Pray, I bless you,
Your Mother

DECEMBER 17

My Dearest Child,

It is only through prayer that you will be able to relate to one another. It is through the love and guidance of the Holy Spirit that this unity will come to be. Be not afraid for you have been chosen. There are no coincidences. Much you do not understand these days. Trust in me and things will become clearer. Stay close to my Son for his love is truth.

Pray, I bless you,
Your Mother

DECEMBER 18

Dear Child,

Stay in prayer my little one and tell them to pray. Tell them I am happy that they've come to pray with me. I will take care of everything for them. They can ask. They can pray with their intentions. They must stay close to me and my Son. All will be well. I am happy they have come; so happy. Pray my little ones.

I bless you,
Your Mother

DECEMBER 19

Dear Child,

There will be many! Show them love and understanding. Be an instrument of peace, so that they may witness the love of my Son, the love of God the Almighty Father through you. It will give them the courage to believe once again that God really does exist and is always present in their lives.

Pray, I bless you,
Your Mother

DECEMBER 20

Dear Child,

In these days of preparation, pray for those in need of a glorious light in the darkness of their souls. As I bring forward my glorious Son their hearts will open with such joy in receiving God himself in the birth of my Son, bringing heavenly light into their world, healing their souls in an instant. Peace on earth! Goodwill to all men!

Rejoice! I love you,
Your Mother

DECEMBER 21

Dear Child,

Tell my dearest shepherds to pray. Tell my dearest shepherds to pick up their weapons against their Goliath. Tell them to pray the rosary before they pray the Holy Mass. For when they do, I will be with them and the Holy Spirit will begin to move in a way that will reach the hearts of many. My Shepherds are the true instruments of peace; the carriers of the love of my Son, Jesus Christ! Tell them how much I love them. Thank them for responding to my call.

Pray, I bless you,
Your Mother

DECEMBER 22

Dear Child,

You are to be the light of joy and peace for others to see. May they see the light of Christ in you, calling their very souls to come forward and wonder in the joy and peace of my heavenly Son as they see it in your face and in your being. Be still and know that it is God who protects you and guides you. Thank you for responding to my call.

Pray, I bless you,
Your Mother

DECEMBER 23

Dear Child,

The joy you feel does not compare to the joy of the angels in heaven as they sing songs of praise to the heavenly Father. All will come to know that he is God the Almighty Father and that he truly does exist. Pray fervently my child. Come follow me. I will lead you to heaven.

Pray, I bless you,
Your Mother

DECEMBER 24

Dear Child,

Remember "Silent night, O Holy Night"? That is what this is; a time of rejoicing in the stillness and peacefulness of God's gift to the world, the Son incarnate. Give praise to my heavenly Father for loving you so much that he gave his only begotten Son, so that sins may be forgiven. O Holy Night is now. Purification of the soul is at your mist. Don't miss the miracle. Love the Lord with all your heart and all your might so that you too may be transformed in his silent night.

Pray, I love you,
Your Mother

DECEMBER 25

Dear Child,

Thank you for all your belief in your heavenly Father even during these times. Know that I carry the child Jesus in my arms today in celebration of his birth! The joy and love being poured on you is unimaginable in your earthly eyes. Know that you are loved here in heaven as you are on earth. The Mass was wonderful, wasn't it? You were right where you were supposed to be, wrapped in my heavenly mantle, being protected by me.

Pray, I bless you,
Your Mother

DECEMBER 26

My Child,

Oh, the Holy Spirit comes upon you in the stillness of the night bringing you joy and peace in your heart. Like the joy of a Mother holding her child, giving glory in everlasting life. Be joyful, give praise for the love I have for my children. I hold them dear to my heart. As a Mother loves her child, so I protect you with my love. Thank you for coming.

Pray, I bless you,
Your Mother

DECEMBER 27

My Dearest Child,

It is you that have now chosen to accept all of the love from my Son. All the love and graces are being poured on you today. Thank you for receiving and accepting the love and joy in your heart. Remember that joy is your birthright! Just remember the birth of my Son. Was that not a glorious moment! In all you do, remember God's heavenly love for you. You will then be able to recognize it in those you love!

Pray, I bless you,
Your Mother

DECEMBER 28

Dear Child,

I am with you. I have always been with you.

I will never leave you,
Your Mother

DECEMBER 29

Dear Child,

Live my messages, live my messages, live my messages upon each waking day. Pray and meditate upon the words and you shall see that my words will become your words and the love of my Son will begin to resonate in your hearts and you will no longer need earthly things to prosper in this world, but the love of my Son will bring glory and goodness and praise in your hearts forever.

I love you,
Your Mother

DECEMBER 30

Dear Child,

You are to be a servant of God, an instrument of his peace and faith. Humble yourself to the Lord, surrender your love to him and as you accept him in your heart more and more each day, the power of God's love and my Son's love will strengthen you in an incredible way! Goodness and praise all the days of your life will be the words you say each and every day! Be happy my child! I smile at you!

Pray, I love you,
Your Mother

DECEMBER 31

Dear Child,

In the peace of the night I come. In the dawn of each morning I'm there by your side watching and protecting your very soul, leading you softly to the arms of the Lord; to the breath of each new day of God's heavenly light. Know that God really does exist and he is everywhere. Pray without ceasing.

I love you,
Your Mother

ACKNOWLEDGMENTS

thank God, the Almighty Father, for allowing our Blessed Mother Mary to come into my heart. I thank Jesus for his most merciful love and patience. Most of all, I thank Our Blessed Mother Mary. Without her persistent love and care, there would be no messages to share. I, too, am thankful for my Mother here on earth who instilled in me the love of the Blessed Mother since I was a little girl. I am forever grateful.

I thank my dear spiritual director, Father Richard Bretone, for his guidance all these years and for encouraging me to publish these divine messages. I also graciously thank all my family and friends, who helped me keep my promise to Our Lady and make this book a reality. I am especially thankful to

Deacon Michael Salvatorelli and all the members of our House of Prayer and for their love of the Blessed Mother Mary. I am so grateful for all their support throughout the years.

I am grateful to Sherry Wachter, author, graphic designer, and writing and literature professor, and Lorraine Ash, author, editor, journalist, and workshop leader. They graciously shared their bountiful wisdom and expertise and helped me achieve the vision for *Mary's Call: The Voice Within Your Soul*.

I am especially thankful to Jeff Ourvan, author, editor, literary agent and founder of The Write Workshop, for his inspiration and belief I could finish and publish this book. I am forever grateful.

ABOUT THE AUTHOR

Linda Morales organizes programs and conferences worldwide for an international trade show association, a position she's held for more than thirty years. Her work has taken her to Europe, Asia, Russia, and South America.

After earning her bachelor's degree in international marketing at Hofstra University, she studied Spanish through the Instituto de San Fernando in Cadíz, Spain. Morales also helped the Instituto develop its programs for foreign students.

Blending her love for travel and devotion to the Blessed Mother Mary, she has visited the Infant Jesus of Prague, the Chapel Rue du Bac (Chapel of Our Lady of the Miraculous Medal) in Paris, and Our Lady of Nations in Amsterdam. Her favorite pilgrimage sites are in Fatima and Medjugorje. Morales has helped organize and lead spiritual retreats and workshops as well as pilgrim groups to various sites.

She is active in her church and house of prayer in her native New York. Her hobbies include reading, writing, crocheting, and playing piano. This is her first book.

Contact Morales at
https://www.lindamorales.com, email:
linda@lindamorales.com
or write to her at P.O. Box 719, Bronx, NY 10465
She can also be reached at
https://www.marysgatheringplace.com.

Made in the USA
Middletown, DE
08 June 2021

41524318R00115